THOUGH THE MOUNTAINS SHAKE

THOUGH THE MOUNTAINS SHAKE

Finding the Refuge We All Need

TERI BENNETT

XULON PRESS

Xulon Press
555 Winderley Pl, Suite 225
Maitland, FL 32751
407.339.4217
www.xulonpress.com

Due to the changing nature of the Internet, if there are any web
addresses, links, or URLs included in this manuscript, these may
have been altered and may no longer be accessible. The views
and opinions shared in this book belong solely to the author and
do not necessarily reflect those of the publisher. The publisher
therefore disclaims responsibility for the views or opinions
expressed within the work.

Unless otherwise indicated, Scripture quotations taken from
the Holy Bible, New Living Translation (NLT). Copyright ©1996,
2004, 2007 by Tyndale House Foundation. Used by permission
of Tyndale House Publishers, Inc.

Cover photo: Mark Bennett

Paperback ISBN-13: 978-1-6628-8764-2

I dedicate this book to

Mark, Graham, Paul and Mari–my family

Kristy, Emily and Kyle–my bigger family

Noah, Amelia, Lucas, Harry, Levi, Caroline, Beau, Rosie, and
Neil–my precious grandkids

And, those who serve others and rebuild hope
in Jesus' Name, especially

Karen, Bindu, Steve, Adam–my church family

Samaritan's Purse

Compassion International

American Red Cross

Habitat for Humanity

The Salvation Army

Convoy of Hope

Doctors Without Borders

Mercy Ships

Catholic Charities

World Vision

Table of Contents

Psalm 46 (NKJV)

"God *is* our refuge and strength,
A very present help in trouble.

Therefore we will not fear,
Even though the earth be removed,
And though the mountains be carried into the midst of the sea;

Though its waters roar *and* be troubled,
Though the mountains shake with its swelling.

There is a river whose streams shall make glad the city of God,
The holy *place* of the tabernacle of the Most High

God *is* in the midst of her, she shall not be moved;
God shall help her, just at the break of dawn.

The nations raged, the kingdoms were moved;
He uttered His voice, the earth melted.

The LORD of hosts *is* with us;
The God of Jacob *is* our refuge.

Come, behold the works of the LORD,
Who has made desolations in the earth.

He makes wars cease to the end of the earth;
He breaks the bow and cuts the spear in two;
He burns the chariot in the fire.

Be still, and know that I *am* God;
I will be exalted among the nations,
I will be exalted in the earth!

The LORD of hosts *is* with us;
The God of Jacob *is* our refuge."

Construction of One World Trade Center, New York City–2011

Introduction

Unbelievable Strength

*T*he crater in the Shanksville field had been filled and flattened. The crash site was undetectable. The hole in the side of the Pentagon was repaired with perfectly-matched stone. The debris from the collapsed towers had been removed. The new tower already reached a height of sixty-six floors.

The three of us–my husband, daughter, and I–were on our last stretch of visiting the crash sites of September 11th. My husband Mark was writing a 10th-anniversary series for our local newspaper.

Each person we met during the week had a September 11th story. However, one man didn't share his "where I was that day" story. Instead, he told what he was doing now, a decade later, at Ground Zero. He introduced himself as a surveyor for the One World Trade Center, being built across the street from where we were standing.

Every story we heard to this point focused on the day the two towers came down. This man's story was about the new, lone tower going up. Our time with him came to mind while I was writing this book.

"This new tower's foundation," he said, "is *unbelievable*."

He described the new skyscraper's foundation and specifications in numbers and exclamation marks. Not being in the construction business, we couldn't appreciate what he was telling us, but his expressions and emphasis showed how astonishing this project had become. Basically, what was going up behind the fence across the street seemed nearly impossible, even to building pros like him.

The concrete used at the site was stronger than most people in the construction industry had ever seen or could imagine.

Super concrete is what it's called. In this surveyor's words, "It's the closest thing to steel."

The conversation that day reminded me of Jesus' parable of the wise man, who built his house foundation on solid rock. This construction surveyor said the goal was to make this the strongest foundation possible, stronger than any building ever made.

It led me to wonder: is it possible to have *faith* as strong as steel?

Faith so strong that no storm, no fire, and no enemy could bring it down?

Does faith like that even exist?

The COVID-19 pandemic made me fearful and anxious in a way I had never felt. It shook my very foundation. The days that led to weeks and months of isolation, cancellations, loss, and depression chipped away at me, little by little. My writing stopped for more than two years.

For weeks and weeks, I felt alone…until I finally went face down in prayer. I needed God to heal what felt broken inside of me.

The Bible says He is my God, and He will strengthen me and help me. He will uphold me with his right hand (Isaiah 41:10).

Strengthen me. Help me. Uphold me. That's what "my God" from Isaiah 41 did for me. He got me up off of the floor.

I needed all of these. *We* all need these–strength, help, lifted up.

Jesus says that *faith* the size of a mustard seed can move mountains. His half-brother James says prayers, offered *in faith,* will make a sick person well. And, the apostle Paul writes that we have been saved, not by our works, but *through faith.*

Trials like COVID pound against us sometimes, over and over again, like storm surges. They make us feel unstable when we're trying to stand. Waves of stress, high and strong, try to consume us. We pray the levees in our life will hold back the danger. Do we have a refuge that will protect us?

Yes!

The Lord is our refuge, He upholds and protects us. With Him, we will not fall.

Imagine not only withstanding the forces of illness, divorce, financial troubles, job struggles, and raising children, but also being strong enough to encourage others through theirs.

The foundation at the One World Trade Center is described as—unbelievable. *Unbelievable.* Yet, it exists. It's mixed, poured, and finished by men. It was invested in by man, built upon by man, and now many rest their lives upon it.

We put our confidence in man all of the time.

Can you imagine what God is capable of building? What we are capable of building with God's leadership?

"For every house has a builder, but the one who built everything is God" (Hebrews 3:4 NLT).

Friend, "we *are* God's house, if we keep our courage, and remain confident in our hope in Christ" (my italics, Hebrews 3:6 NLT).

If. If we keep our courage. If we remain confident and if we cling to our hope in Christ.

What do you do when life hits you hard? How confident are you in those tough times? Do you remain hopeful?

The surveyor working at Ground Zero lit up when talking about what he witnessed at the construction site. He saw the towers come down on the television the same as many of us. However, he was excited to be part of the building process.

I want to captivate listeners when I tell my story of how Jesus repaired my heart and thinking, and how He's rebuilt my life after some pretty intense blows. And, I get excited to be part of helping other followers build their faith and tell their own story. I want to be engaged in the building process, not be a spectator.

Often we pray that God makes us his hands and feet or a tool in his hand. Either way, we aren't in charge. He is. We simply become laborers.

Being part of God's crew means we will perform a wide variety of tasks wherever He takes us and with the strength He gives us.

My deepest hope when you read this book is that you make God your first place to turn. Not your second, third, or last. Make him your refuge and strength. God–the greatest architect and creator–has also uniquely designed you, and his love for you is put into every detail. Brick by brick.

The Father will strengthen your faith, deepen it, and make it the source of your courage, confidence, and hope.

Each chapter of this book builds upon the other, starting under the surface. Together, we will see how God's plan for you is ready, and once you commit to Him, He will break ground and transform you.

It's time–to stand *on* your faith. To put your full weight and trust upon that foundation.

Don't imagine what God could build upon that. He already has. May your new, first instincts be to turn to Him in your weakness. In the chaos. Let Him be your refuge. And, in turn, give God permission to move into your heart and test your strength in the trials. Watch your faith become unbelievably strong–from the ground up!

I'm in this with you,
Teri Bennett

Samaritan's Purse Rebuild, New Orleans, LA–2010

Chapter 1

His Plans

> "'For I know the plans I have for you,' declares the Lord,
> 'plans to prosper you and not harm you.
> Plans for hope and a future.'"
> Jeremiah 29:11 (NIV)

I read those words every morning and every evening before I went to sleep. Someone before me had written them in Sharpie on the foot of my bunk bed.

Nearly sixty of us spent a week in New Orleans, not to celebrate Mardi Gras or vacation in The Big Easy, but to rebuild homes after Hurricane Katrina. Many families were, five years later, still trying to get back in their homes.

Our team stayed in a church in the 8th Ward. We worked on homes during the day and stayed at the church in the evening. Women bunked on one side of the church and men on the other. Each room housed more than a dozen beds.

After setting up my sleeping area, I spotted Jeremiah 29:11 scrawled on my bed frame.

Throughout the week, that verse not only had me thinking about the plans God had for me, but also for the others on the trip and the homeowners we were serving.

In Chapter 29 of the book of Jeremiah, the prophet Jeremiah writes to the exiled people of Jerusalem. The Babylonian soldiers had come to Jerusalem, torn down its walls and destroyed its city and temple. Following King Nebuchadnezzar's orders, the king's men captured the city's best–its strong, smart, and young. The prophet Jeremiah, who was left behind, writes a letter to the captives telling them what God has specifically spoken to him.

These people, called "God's Remnant," are living under King Nebuchadnezzar's rule in Babylon. In Jeremiah's letter, they are instructed how to live, work, and pray, right where they are. God has promised them, through Jeremiah, that He listens to their prayers and will end their captivity in seventy years.

Seventy years.

Have you ever had what you know uprooted or turned end over end? Have you doubted anything good could come of your situation?

The Lord says through Jeremiah to the people of Israel that his plans are for them to stay. God wants his people to build homes, marry, have children, plant fields, work, and pray for the welfare of the city where they are (verses 4-14).

Jeremiah assures them in his letter that God has a plan for them, and upon it, He is establishing something. Something greater, and they as his people are going to prosper.

In the middle of our own despair, God just may be doing something we don't understand.

We must be patient and trust Him. I admit, that's not easy for me. Especially the patient part.

How many years would it be before God would deliver his people? Seventy? Seventy years is a lifetime. Most of this Remnant wouldn't live long enough to see the outcome. Nonetheless, one is coming.

Like the Remnant in Babylon, others in the Bible didn't live to see God's plan to completion. Moses, Aaron, David, John the Baptist. They were all part of the plan, an important part, but their role was to move God's plan forward. Their crossing the finish line wasn't God's goal.

We ourselves may not see a plan of God's to completion, but God will complete it. We may be just a segment of it, getting it closer to God's ultimate goal. Time is a limitation for us, but not for God.

The English teacher in me recognizes the word *plan* as both a noun and a verb. In Hebrew, when "plan" is a noun, it's *machashbah* – meaning a thought, plan, or invention. Its verb form, *chashab*, is to think, invent, or imagine.[1]

Interestingly, we can't *have* a plan until we plan. We can't *have* the noun until we go through the action, or verb, first. One must think, invent, imagine, or plan *before* a plan exists. Inventing comes *before* the invention, thinking *before* the thought, and creating *before* the creation. Once again, the act of planning comes first.

In Jeremiah's letter, God tells his people that the planning stage is done, and God *has* plans for them…to make them—his chosen nation through Abraham—something new.

For us, God has plans, too, and his planning is complete. Done. He's now building upon that plan.

Let's consider the first plan God ever established for us.

3

Genesis Chapters 1-2 tells the creation story. In the first verse, God didn't start with creating man. Scripture explains how God took nothingness and chaos to create a world for man (and woman) to live. Creator God formed the heavens and earth, day and night, the land and seas, stars and celestial objects. Man wasn't formed before the fish and birds and all the wild animals. God created all of these before He established man.

In his perfect plan, God built a place for man to live, with light and stars to guide him, water and vegetation and fruit to feed him, and food to sustain every living creature. Looking over his creation each day, God saw "it was very good!"

Recently, spectacular images from the James Webb Space Telescope began transmitting back to NASA, and parts of the universe have been seen for the first time. Have you seen these images? If not, look them up online. I look at them in awe, and I marvel at the universe's beauty, and how much we've never seen. When I look up at the sky and think of those images, I wonder, *How could anyone question a Creator?*

Do you do that? Look at a sunrise or sunset, the ocean or fall foliage changes, and see it's "very good"? Do you think to thank God for his perfect order of a perfect creation?

It wasn't until all this was established, that God "formed man from the dust of the ground." He THEN breathed the "breath of life into the man's nostrils, and the man became a living person" (Genesis 2:7 NIV).

I'm particularly fond of the *Message* version of Ephesians on God's plan for us from the beginning. Consider reading Chapter 1 in its entirety. The apostle Paul writes, "Long before [God] laid earth's foundations, he had us in mind…He thought of everything, provided for everything we could possibly need." Creator God, Elohim, thought of everything we would need and THEN established it. Paul says long before creation, He had us *in mind*. Verb before noun. Creating *before* creation.

God focuses on our needs *and* his purposes.

We are the "focus of his love." He delighted in making the plans that would set us free. "Long, long ago he decided to adopt us into his family through Jesus Christ," and it's *through* Christ we get to learn God's long-range plan for everyone and everything (v. 3-10 MSG).

Again, time is not an issue for God. *Long, long* ago and *long-range* plans are terms only we measure.

The apostle Paul begins the book of Ephesians, "I, Paul, am under God's plan." He writes that he is called by the Lord to bring everyone, but especially Gentiles, to Christ.

Paul interjects, "What pleasure [God] took in planning this!" (v. 3-6 MSG).

Like Paul, we too **can** have a clear focus and see exactly what God is calling us – his followers – to do (v. 13-19 MSG).

When our family committed to serving in New Orleans in 2010, we didn't know exactly what to expect, but we trusted God. If He wanted us to go, He would have to clear the way.

So, we turned it over to the Lord.

King Solomon writes in Proverbs 16:3 (NIV), "Commit to the LORD whatever you do, and he will establish your plans."

Commit in the Bible means to "roll it over" or "put it upon." My husband, daughter, and I handed our schedules, funds, and family arrangements over to him, and He made a way.

Obstacles that we thought might thwart our trip were nowhere to be found, and we felt encouraged and eager to serve. So, we went, according to God's plan—as part of the church body--to rebuild and love on hurting families.

In the latter part of his ministry, Jesus talks to his disciples of God's plan–to establish or build his church body–and Peter, who professes his faith in Jesus as the Messiah, is to be "the rock" the church body will be built upon.

Matthew 16:13-19 (NIV) says that the body of the church cannot ever be conquered or thwarted, and no powers in hell will ever tear that down. Jesus is building his church, the body of Christ, according to God's plan on solid rock.

When Jesus tells his disciples of his coming arrest, torture, and death, Peter vows to keep that from happening and to protect Jesus. Jesus rebukes Peter, in fact, for getting in the way of God's plan which is to redeem his followers of their sin.

"Jesus turned and said to Peter, 'Get behind me, Satan! You are a stumbling block to Me; you do not have in mind the concerns of God, for you are not setting your mind on God's interests, but man's.'" v. 23 (NASB)

Have you ever thought of that? You could be getting in God's way?

Just as God is in the process of building, inventing, or creating something new in his people while they are away in Babylon and just as Christ is creating a body of believers through his disciples, He is also "creating something new" in each of us. He is using the Holy Spirit—right where we are—in all of our mess, all of our chaos, all of our storms, and all of our suffering. God can clear the debris or walk with us through it, if we ask Him.

God has planned the way for those who have said "yes" to making Him Lord of their life, and He doesn't just have one plan either. Jeremiah 29:11 says the Lord has "plans."

Skip Moen (author, professor, speaker, and dean at Master's International Divinity School) says, "God does not have one perfect plan for us. He has one purpose — one goal — that you become all you were meant to be through conforming to the image of the Messiah. The goal never changes. But the plans are new ideas every day."[2]

I love what Moen says--that God's goal for us never changes. For us to become all we are meant to be--means conforming to the image of Christ.

God can work through our issues. Our conflicts won't get in his way. *We* may get in his way, and sometimes we need to step aside to let him carry out his plan.

Following Jesus doesn't mean we will be free from troubles or issues. God may just *allow* trying and heartbreaking times to happen, if only to teach or shape us and to test us and our faith. He doesn't do it out of malice for us. That's not God.

Jeremiah wrote that God's plan is "not to harm us."

Life is messy, painful and heavy, but in spite of it all, God is in it with us. He's for us, He's in charge, and He offers us hope and a future.

Hope. That's what keeps most of us going. It keeps us from quitting.

God declares He has hope and plans for his exiled people in Babylon, and He offers us hope, too. He has hopes *and* plans for us, and that's all we need to cling to—grace and hope.

We don't have to wonder if God loves us or if He would lead us astray. We don't have to fear He will walk away when we mess up or challenge Him. He won't start something in us that He won't finish. God loves us so much that He *planned* a way for us to be redeemed, and then He carried out that plan—He sent his one and only Son to make us victorious over sin and make us holy.

If. We. Accept. Him.

Therefore, we must first *commit to the LORD all that we do*, unconditionally; placing upon Him all our concerns and trusting Him in that commitment; and then wait. Wait on the Lord. Commit first. Then wait. *He will establish our plans.*

I invite you to say this prayer with me:

Heavenly Father, I realize you are more than I will ever know. You created all, and that includes me. Nothing about you or this universe is random. All is according to your plan. You are the Lord of all. You prepared a way for me, and you will follow it to completion. I don't want to stand in the way. Give me a willing heart to follow where your Spirit leads me even through my mess. I want to know your plans for my life. Build me up, Lord. Amen

Application: Get Out of God's Way

Our older son Graham called on a Sunday evening. I could hear panic in his voice. He was hundreds of miles away at a new job in Pittsburgh, and his car axle broke, literally leaving him without wheels. I immediately went into parent-to-the-rescue mode.

Wouldn't most parents?

My husband Mark and I decided to drive our truck to Pittsburgh, leave it if needed, and we had a car loan pre-approved, should our son need to make a quick purchase. All of our plans seemed to solve his problem, and we were ready to head out...until he called the next day. Graham talked to his company about his situation, they gave him a company car for as long as he needed, and his demeanor was 180° from the night before.

Problem solved...and *we had nothing to do with it.*

We had a plan to take care of our son, when all along God was intervening on his behalf. God had a plan for Graham, too. A better plan. Afterwards, I felt God was telling me, "Do you trust me with your son?"

My husband and I had committed to teaching Graham, even before he was born, who God is and how to trust Him. But, we didn't let God take the wheel in this situation. (No pun intended).

We had to get out of the way for God to show Graham who he really needed to lean on. We needed a reminder as well. God showed us how He has established himself in our son's life and is with him.

The Contemporary English Version of Proverbs 16:1 reads, "We humans make plans, but the LORD has the final word."

Consider these questions:

- What plans, or commitments, have YOU said *yes* to in the past week?
- Did anything come along that may have altered or canceled those plans?
- In hindsight, how did you react to those changes in your plans?
- Is there a possibility that God's plan was something different for you?

Sure, there's that possibility.

Romans 8:28 (NLT) reads, "God causes everything to work together for the good of those who love God and are called according to his purpose [or plan] for them." With God, all things are possible. He is for you, not against you. God's direction for you may not be what you would envision, but you can't know what lies ahead if you don't trust Him and let Him take the wheel.

We can get in his way sometimes or become bitter that plans didn't go as we hoped. Remember, his plans are not to hurt us, but to see us have hope and a future.

In addition to his Word, God may include Spirit-led people like Jeremiah who can help you to understand or navigate his plan for you. These people may be insightful enough or wise enough to see what you do not.

- Is there anyone around you, who actively pursues Christ, whom you could lean on for godly guidance?
- Could you possibly be that person for someone else?

- Who is one person you could *commit* to praying for and *commit* to helping grow closer to Christ?

Insert the name of that person in each blank below.

"'For I know the plans I have for _____,' declares the Lord, 'plans to prosper _____ and not harm _____. Plans for hope and a future.'"

Now read it aloud and finish with "Amen".

Commit this to your prayers, and then get out of the way. Wait patiently to see what God does.

Rewrite Jeremiah 29:11. However, this time, where there is a blank, insert YOUR name.

_____

_____

_____

_____

_____

_____

_____

When your plans don't go as you intended this week, look around to see where God may be working in your situation. Be patient. His answers are not always immediate.

Ephesians 1:1 (MSG) begins, "I, Paul, am under God's plan." Paul commits himself to the Lord and all that he is doing. He submits himself to the Father's will.

Read that verse again below, but this time, insert your name in the blank:

"I, _____, am under God's plan ..."

Ask yourself:

- Have I committed to, or put upon, the Lord everything I am doing?
- Have I considered God has a plan already in motion for me?
- Am I getting in God's way of his establishing those plans?

Put this verse to memory this week: Proverbs 16:3 (NIV)

"Commit to the LORD whatever you do, and He will establish your plans."

Photo by Nancy Padan
Fairbanks Park, Terre Haute, Indiana–2018

Chapter Two

Preparation

"Prepare your work outside;
get everything ready for yourself in the field,
and after that build your house."
Proverbs 24:27 (ESV)

I spied little footprints in the sidewalk. Not *on* the sidewalk. *In* the sidewalk.

Something had obviously walked in the wet cement when the sidewalk was freshly poured. The paw prints blocked my way, figuratively speaking. By my guess, a cat did this.

Anyone seeing me leaning over and studying the concrete might have thought, "*What* is she doing?"

I finally moved on, finished my walk, got in my car, and headed home.

All the way home, I wondered to myself why that caught my attention. I had walked this stretch dozens of times and not noticed it.

Often, I ask God to show me what He wants me to see—whether it's on a mission trip, studying scripture, writing, or obviously strolling a sidewalk.

So, thinking about the imprints in the sidewalk, I asked, "What was that all about, Lord?"

For whatever reason, I pondered over this for several days. I returned to it a few times and even took pictures of it, though I didn't know why.

I wish sometimes God would make sense of things. You know what I mean? He has a plan for me. That I understand, and He's creating something new in me through that plan. That part excites me. But, *why do I find myself noticing little things like these paw prints and looking for their significance?*

Maybe I don't need to know, or maybe God will reveal it to me later. Maybe there *is* no point. Still, here I am—talking to God about them and asking Him.

Connections happen often when I read scripture. I may be reading something I've seen many times, but on one particular time, a word or verse that never really stood out before suddenly grabs my eye. It has significance to what I'm experiencing at that time in my life, and now suddenly it has personal meaning. It feels as though God is saying something about himself or me.

This one concrete sidewalk that I amble beside this one particular river in Indiana is insignificant, yet it serves a purpose. It gets walkers like me from one end of this park to the other. A small thing–a sidewalk, right?

My life, in the scope of the whole universe, may seem no more significant than a few cat pawprints in a short stretch of Indiana sidewalk. Yet, here I am, and so are you… It may *seem* by the scale of the universe, one person—one life—can't really be too significant.

Author Frank White wrote in his book, *The Overview Effect: Space Exploration and Human Evolution*, that astronauts who saw the earth from space had an experience that made the existence of man and the Earth seem so precious and fragile. William Shatner, Captain Kirk of *Star Trek* fame, said seeing the earth from the window of his short, Origin Blue "space" flight made him sob deeply.

White reports astronauts return with a grander feeling of the universe and a smaller feeling of self.

Neil Armstrong in the Apollo 11 flight looked at the earth, covered it with his thumb, and came to the realization that he wasn't a giant. In fact, he was very, very small.[3]

However, 2,000 years ago a man from humble beginnings walked the earth, taught thousands, healed hearts and bodies, and occupied time and space for thirty-three years. He dirtied his feet walking with and telling others of the grace of God. He talked to the sickly, unwanted, and undesirable. He was the scapegoat for the whole world and carried the very cross He would be crucified upon. He died for the sins of every man, woman, and child, then and today, and He rose from the grave— just as He said He would. He changed the world for me. For you. His name is Jesus.

How much does one person really matter? How much do you or I matter? Let's consider the planning and preparation involved in paving the way in a person's life.

First, the planning...

As a little girl watching Grandpa help Dad pour a concrete driveway, I didn't realize that preparation is the most important aspect of pouring a concrete slab. Their plan was to pour half of it on one Saturday and the other half the next weekend. However, they had the big job of preparing the area beforehand.

Now, the prepping...

The whole process stretched over several days. I caught glimpses of this ambitious duo cutting the perimeter with a spade where the driveway would go. They drove wooden stakes in the ground and wrapped string around them, a few inches above the dirt.

Together, they dug up the sod, tossed it all in the bed of Dad's truck, and cleared the area of all grass and roots. Two-by-fours were made into a perimeter frame. Dirt clods were broken up using a spade, before leveling the ground with a rake. Finally, they tamped down the area making it a hard, smooth surface on which to pour the concrete.

All of this took time. The ground had to be ready because there would be no time to prep once the cement mixer started churning out concrete.

When most people look at a concrete slab, all they see is the surface, the part they walk on. The planning and preparation that go into the concrete are unrecognized, but actually *that* is where most of the work is done.

Every time I read Matthew Chapter 1 or Luke Chapter 3, I realize that each of the people in Jesus' bloodline was part of God's plan, as was each Old Testament prophet–major and minor–preparation for the coming of our Savior Christ.

Most people look at Christians the same way. All they see is on the surface. People don't know all of the planning and preparing God has done and is still doing inside of a follower of Christ. We may never know what people before us did to prepare a way for us.

God is not only prepared for what we will face in life. He is also way ahead of us. He's already paved the way.

In the book of Exodus, the story has many turns and twists.

The Hebrew people have been enslaved for more than 400 years. Like the captives in Babylon, God's people have prayed for generations that He will rescue them. God tells Moses He has heard the cries of his people, and He's *prepared* for Moses to lead them out of Egypt and bondage. The plan is made, and Moses is God's deliverer.

Egypt's pharaoh is obstinate. He doesn't make the task easy for Moses. Ten times, God shows his power and strength to not only Pharaoh, but also the enslaved Hebrews. A river of blood, plagues of frogs and gnats, diseased livestock, skin boils, hailstorms, locusts and darkness bring death, destruction, and fear. The final blow to Pharaoh–the death of his own son– crushes Pharaoh's own hardened heart. In this moment, Pharaoh, overwhelmed in his personal loss, sends God's people away with Moses.

"Get out!" he orders. "Leave my people—and take the rest of the Israelites with you!" (Exodus 12:31 NLT).

The Lord is not only *with* Moses and the Israelites but He also goes on *ahead* of them, guiding them day and night by a light (and cloud).

Pharaoh's heart hardens once again, and the Egyptian ruler takes his army after the Israelites, chasing them to the edge of the Red Sea. "I have planned this," God tells Moses, "in order to display my glory through Pharaoh and his whole army" (Exodus 14:4, NLT).

When Pharaoh's army hems God's people in between them and the Red Sea, God opens up the sea and makes a way for all of his people to cross to the other side.

In Exodus, Joshua, Psalms, Corinthians, and Hebrews, the Bible reminds us of the dry ground beneath the Israelites' feet as they crossed the sea. "Your way was through the sea, your path through the great waters, yet your footprints were unseen" (Psalm 77:19 ESV). The ground was bone dry.

There won't be any footprints or paw prints left behind. God has paved the way, and it is dry ground.

"When [Moses and] the people…saw the mighty power that the LORD had unleashed…they were **filled with awe** before him" and they put their faith in the Lord and the one He chose to lead them (my emphasis, Exodus 14:31 NLT).

The paw prints I saw in the concrete slab in the park captured my attention for a moment. Imagine the reaction of God's people walking between walls of water and across the dry bottom of the sea. The Egyptian soldiers are on the heels of the Hebrew people. How do the Hebrews feel? Captivated? God's people are *filled with awe*!

God commands Moses to "get moving!" as He divides the Red Sea. *Two million* Israelites walk across the dry sea floor! Not muddy, not covered in plants or coral or sea life. Dry ground. God has gone before them and prepared their path.

Even when you may be frozen in fear because the enemy is upon you, God may tell you to *keep moving*! What God did for Moses and his people He will do for you and me. He will rescue us from impossible situations and have a way out we don't expect. What we see as impossible, to God is more than possible—He's already done it!

The Lord our God—Creator, Protector, and Provider—crosses before us all of the time. He's already ahead of us. This side of heaven, we won't know the many times God has walked before us, guided and led us, and gotten between us and forces intent to harm us. What proof or evidence do we have that it is God directing our life?

When we have faith, we don't need footprints, evidence, or something concrete to believe. "Faith makes us sure of what we hope for and gives us proof of what we cannot see" (Hebrews 11:1 CEV).

I admit, my eyes have wanted to see Christ. My heart has wanted to see Jesus working through the tragedy of the storm. I've wanted to see for myself the footprints, tablets, ark, and shroud. Still, without this evidence, do I say to others I've found Christ? You bet I do.

Mission trips *fill me with awe*. I've seen volunteers come from places far and wide to help total strangers. Like me, they say they felt drawn by something inside of them. Can I say I've seen Christ on my trips? Not in body and physical form, but in Spirit and love. I see the love of Jesus in those who come to serve others in their time of need.

Has anyone ever come to your rescue or service? A total stranger? Has anyone ever paid your bill, carried your weight, or said an unexpected kind word to you? This may very well be from the Father.

Keep your eyes, ears, heart, and mind open to any way the Lord may be speaking to you, showing himself to you. It may not be bold. It may not be loud. It may not be bright or fiery. It may be just a quiet whisper or small footprints in concrete that work on your faith and make you think of Him. You may find yourself doing something you otherwise wouldn't, something *you* didn't plan, and you just may say you saw Jesus in it.

I invite you to join me in this prayer:

Heavenly Father, Preparer and Provider, You've planned and paved a way for all who've chosen to follow You. You walk before me and with me. Give me courage to walk where I have never gone before. May my eyes see things that remind me of You and keep me confident and hopeful for what You have in store. In all things I pray, Amen

Application: I Know Your Name

**"My sheep listen to my voice; I know them,
and they follow me."
John 10:27 (NIV)**

I think most of us would recognize the writing or signature of our parents, spouse, children, and closest friends. Why? Because we've spent a great deal of time with them. We've seen their handwriting on cards, notes, lists, etc. We know their writing's unique characteristics and even its voice.

We don't have to see God's signature in our life or Jesus' footprints to recognize their work. That is, if we've spent much time with them. Being in God's Word, listening to the teachings of Christ, and spending time in prayer make us familiar with the sound of their voice and their hand upon our life. We just know. Just as your fingerprints, DNA, and voice are unique to you, so is your name to God.

Write your signature.

_____

- Name different times you are *required* to provide your signature.
- When was a time you did something kind for someone, but you didn't leave your name—you did it anonymously?
- Were you *required* to keep it anonymous?
- How does it feel, doing something kind without leaving "your mark"?

Matthew 6:3 reads,

> "...when you give to someone in need, don't let your left hand know what your right hand is doing." (NIV)

Read Matthew 6:4.

The "someone in need" whom you do something for may never know it was you. You do it and move on. Like paying for someone's bill anonymously or offering a perfect stranger help and then walking away. God will know. He sees your faith by what you do. Your great reward comes *later*, in heaven. He has prepared that for you. It. Is. Yours.

Keep what you did between you and the Father. He doesn't need your signature. He knows.

God has prepared many things for you. Some you will not know of maybe till you meet Him face to face. But, trust He is working for you.

For sure, Jesus has prepared a way for your name to be recorded in a heavenly way–in the Lamb's Book of Life. If your name is written in the Lamb's Book of Life, He will NEVER erase it nor change his plans. You are set free! One day, He will announce to the Father that you are his (Revelation 3:5).

You. Are. His.

Write your name on the top line. Then, list names of others you hope are in the Lamb's Book of Life.

_____	_____
_____	_____
_____	_____
_____	_____
_____	_____

Did you run out of lines? I hope so.

Pray for each of the names above—yours included. This step is in preparation of what's to come. These people may not know you are praying for them, but do it anyway. You don't have to tell them. However, God's listening. Ask Him to reveal himself to you and to these other people in ways, big or small.

I'm praying, too, that you are *filled with so much awe* by what you learn that you are led to build something truly worthy of the King.

Morgan and Carli
Photo by Staci Tryon, 360 Chicago–2022

Chapter Three

A Strong Foundation

"Let your roots grow down into him, and let your lives
be built on him." Colossians 2:7 (NLT)

A handful of people tilted over The Magnificent Mile
in the skyscraper's glass attraction. Others took pictures of themselves sitting on a glass-enclosed ledge extending
out of the building.

875 North Michigan Avenue, formerly called the John
Hancock Center, has a 360° view of the city of Chicago. The
dark exterior with its "X" beams has become a recognizable
structure worldwide.

Something most people may not know about the tower is:
It almost failed.

The Michigan Avenue high-rise has a unique look that took
years to build, from groundbreaking to setting the two antennas
on top. Like all buildings, this skyscraper's ability to manage
stress had to be calculated. The possibility of facing strong
winds and earthquake forces was considered in its design.

Why?

Stress is inevitable.

Stress is the result of pressure or tension placed upon something. In life, like in buildings, we can plan on stress, but we aren't always prepared for it.

Everyone experiences stress. Yet, how we each handle the pressure or tension will determine if we (like a building) are still standing when the storm winds pass.

Everyone—kids included—struggles with stress from emotional strain, demanding circumstances, and physical suffering. Together and individually, these add to what we are already carrying. Stress piles upon stress.

No one needs to be told that stress can be overwhelming. We all know that, right?

Got kids? Major stress.

Married? Oh yeah. Stress too.

Have a job? Hours and hours of stress.

It was stress that brought the Chicago skyscraper's construction to a halt for six months and could have brought it down to a pile of rubble had a problem not been detected. The *Chicago Tribune* reported that the loss to the city, if the building had not been built, would have paled in comparison to "the cost in dollars or in lives [if stress] damage might have befallen the 100-story John Hancock Center."[4] It's unimaginable what could happen if the building had failed. Reporter Bob Hughes stated the thought was "just too horrible to dwell upon."

What brought this project to a halt? A flaw in its foundation that couldn't handle the stress placed upon it.

The foundation of the John Hancock Center began like all skyscrapers–a plan was formed. (Remember, the verb first. Then, the noun.) All the logistics—design, engineering, materials, contractors, etc.—were selected and hired, and ground was broken for what some thought would be "architectural innovation" in Chicago. Instead, because of its foundation failure, it became "the most thoroughly studied structure in the history of the construction industry."[5] Failure, undoubtedly, wasn't in the builders' plan.

"Like the roots of a tree, a skyscraper's foundation is laid below ground to create the most stability."[6] Building the monumental John Hancock Center, of course, began below ground. A concrete "root system," much like a tree's, was created in the ground for foundational support. Most of the supports of this building went down as much as 200 feet till they met bedrock. The other supports went down 88 feet until they met unbroken ground.

However, when weight was placed on the base of the foundation, a worker spotted a problem. The structure began to tilt. It was unstable.[7]

Construction on this project had to stop immediately. Testing had to be done. Inspections and repairs took time and cost the project an additional $1 million.

The cause? Flaws in the foundation and debris that shouldn't have been there.

What if the defects hadn't been discovered and fixed? What if the building had risen hundreds, and even a thousand feet, and then it failed? The damage and loss could have been unimaginable.[8]

The foundation of a building bears its load. It's the bottom, or the base, that something else is built and rests upon.

Our faith requires a strong foundation as well. It's what we build our decisions, thoughts, words, and actions upon. Our very life and eternity rest upon it. When the weight, temptation, and stress of life test us, we need to know, with certainty, that we will still be standing. We need to know our foundation is stable and will hold.

Jesus gives us that certainty. He concludes his Sermon on the Mount telling the crowd that his teachings are the foundation we need to build and rest our faith upon. He says, "Anyone who listens to my teachings and follows it is wise, like a person who builds a house on solid rock" (Matthew 7:24 NLT).

Another word for stability is resilience. *Resilience* is how something—or someone—continues standing or bounces back from stress or pressure. A person's resilience cannot likely be seen on the outside. It often comes from within.

Did you ever sing the Sunday school song "The Wise Man Built His House Upon the Rock"? The simple tune emphasizes what a wise man does (builds his house upon the rock) and compares that to what a foolish man does (builds his house upon the sand). When both houses experience a storm, heavy rains come, and consequently, so do the floods. The two houses' durability through the storm says something about the two men who built them.

When storms arise in our life (and they will) and when floods and wind "beat against the house," Jesus concludes, "[our faith] won't collapse." Stress, oppression, and storms of life—all will hammer away at us—but if we put our trust in the Lord, He will make us resilient, and we will not falter. His strength is greater than any storm, and He will get us through.

We *will* stand firm.

Well, if that song became an earworm for you, you may have continued singing it in your head, and you know "the house on the rock stood firm" whereas the "house on the sand went *splat!*" The lesson of the song, the lesson of Jesus' message in Matthew, and the lesson in building the John Hancock Center are the same—pay particular attention to your foundation because it's where you place your trust.

The children's song concludes that if you "build your house on the Lord Jesus Christ… the blessings will come down as your prayers go up!"

When you face the stress that comes with storms in life, what's the first thing you do? Do you flee, lash out, or do you pray? When the world seems to be tilting under the weight of stress, do you holler for help or fall to pieces? When someone asks where your strength comes from, what do you say?

We cannot put our hope in our job, our investments, those people in positions of authority, or even our kids because those all can tilt or fail. Faith in Christ is all we have that assuredly will not crumble, and on Him we can rest all of our weight.

In Psalm 62:2 (NIV), David says, "Truly [the Lord] is my rock and my salvation." David knows, like the man who builds his house upon the rock, that God will remain steadfast and faithful to him, through the challenges and storms. Because of his faith, David is a strong tower (even as a young boy) and will never be shaken.

The biggest buildings in this world—those concrete Goliaths—can come down because of strong winds, turbulent waters, and earthquake forces. Ironically, small flaws also have the potential to bring down tall towers, such as the one in Chicago, and it can cost dearly.

Throughout his life, David experiences overwhelming stress and adversity before and during his reign over Israel. Bears, lions, giants, kings, and soldiers all see David as a threat to what they want, and yet he is well-equipped, or built, for the fight. Just as a rock in a slingshot brings the great Philistine soldier

Goliath to the ground, David knows a greater rock exists that is his refuge and his strength.

David fights when the Lord tells him to fight, and he abstains when he doesn't have God's blessing. At times, he fights on high ground; and other times, he flees into caves. Yet, David cries out in Psalm 62:5 (NIV), "Yes, my soul, find rest in God; he is my mighty rock, my refuge."

The Lord is David's foundation—his rock.

What do you have as your foundation? Is your soul at rest? To whom or what do you cry out when you need strength? What tries to steal your peace?

Some people foolishly view themselves as tall towers—nothing can bring them down. They believe they physically, intellectually, financially, or even spiritually stand on their own.

The apostle Paul writes in I Corinthians 10:12 (WE), "Therefore, when a person thinks, 'I am strong; I can stand,' let that person be careful, or he will fall." Paul sounds like he knows a little something about engineering. He knows the power and strength of God.

Like engineers who know about anchoring a skyscraper, arborists know what makes a well-anchored tree. Scott Jamieson of Bartlett Tree Research Laboratories says, "So much of a tree's health and stability depends on its roots."[2] Jamieson is talking about a tree's foundation. A tree with healthy roots thrives, and one with a diseased or damaged root system will struggle to survive. It, too, just might tilt when faced with winds, floods, and stress.

California redwood trees, for example, are some of the tallest and oldest trees in the world. They can measure over 350 feet tall and live more than 1,000 years. You might expect such Goliaths to have a deep root system to anchor a tree of that size.

However, unlike buildings of concrete and steel, throughout the world, these majestic "skyscrapers" have a root system only 5 or 6 feet deep.

How do they stay so stable?

Though redwoods have shallow root systems, their roots spread out over 100 feet, these trees grow in clusters, and they intertwine their wide root system by anchoring with others like them. In other words, redwoods live in community. They support each other—at the foundation—and that allows them to be well-supported, grow tall, and grow wide. "This increases their stability during strong winds and floods."[10]

The apostle Paul tells how valuable relationships rooted in faith and community are. He tells the people of Corinth, "[T]here should be no division in the body, but that its parts should have equal concern for each other" (I Corinthians 12:25, NIV). We, as a church, should live like redwoods—if one tree suffers, those close to it in the cluster will also; and if one thrives, so will the others. In the church, we are "the body of Christ, and each one of you is a part of it" (I Corinthians 12:27 NIV).

We must remember the importance of maintaining our connections with other believers, to ensure our community thrives. We have a responsibility to each other. The more we spread our roots and intertwine with others doing the same, the stronger we all are anchored. Following the Lord means strengthening our faith, as well as each other's faith.

Skyscrapers don't share foundations. They don't share each other's weight. They don't support one another when storms come or floods arise. They aren't strengthened by one another. They may be geographically *part of* a community but they don't *live in* community with one another.

If Christ is your Lord and Savior, you have Him indwelling you. You are the temple of God.

The apostle Paul says, "Christ may dwell in your hearts through faith—that you, being rooted and grounded in love, may have strength" (Ephesians 3:16-19 ESV). That strength is your anchor during the storm, and no storm can rip you from the foundation Christ has given you.

However, the word *may* in the verse above puts the weight of the decision on you. Jesus doesn't force himself onto anyone. You choose. If you choose to anchor yourself in God's grace and love, you won't be standing on your own strength, but His.

Let your roots grow deep in Him, and He will uphold you.

I invite you to pray with me:

Heavenly Father, I often feel fearful because I lose trust in the ground that I stand on. I fear failure, pain, humility, and loss, but I chose to hand over to you all that shakes up my mind and heart. Put me on solid ground–the foundation of the prophets and apostles...and You, Christ Jesus. I chose to commit what I am doing to Your will and trust Your ways. Give me courage to open my eyes. Amen

Photo by Carla Wehrmeyer
Redwood National Park, California–2015

Application: The Roots of Stability

If you were asked to draw a tree, would you think to include the roots that grow unseen and underground?

In Ephesians 3:17-19 (NLT), Paul writes that through the Holy Spirit, Christ will make his home in your heart, and

"Your roots will grow down into God's love and keep you strong."

Although you usually cannot see a tree's root system, it still exists and has a purpose. Tree roots not only soak up the water and nutrients from the ground, they also anchor the tree and hold it up.

God's love will feed *you* as the soil does the tree. It will strengthen you as a foundation does a building. Paul goes on to say how much he prays we know the extent God really does love us—how wide, how long, how high, and how deep our Father in Heaven's love is.

Name as many different parts of a tree as you can.

_____   _____

_____   _____

_____   _____

_____   _____

_____   _____

Name as many different types of trees as you can.

_____ _____

_____ _____

_____ _____

_____ _____

_____ _____

Who created all of these parts and types of trees?

_____

How are *all* of these trees strengthened and anchored?

_____

If God made all of these trees and all of their parts and God takes care of all of them, what do you have to worry about? God loves you so much that he sent his Son, Jesus, to die for you so that you may be forgiven of your sins and live with Him in eternity. On that truth, we can stand.

Name those people, whom you believe are rooted in Christ, that are or would make a good support system for you.

1. _____
2. _____
3. _____
4. _____
5. _____

How could *you* be a better support system for others? What encouragement could you offer others to feed their soul?

_____

_____

_____

Reflection song: Make this hymn by Edward Motes a prayer for yourself, those with whom you are in community, and those you can strengthen by your own faith.

"My Hope is Built on Nothing Less"

"My hope is built on nothing less
than Jesus' blood and righteousness;
I dare not trust the sweetest frame,
but wholly lean on Jesus' name.

Refrain:
On Christ, the solid rock, I stand;
all other ground is sinking sand,
all other ground is sinking sand.

When darkness veils his lovely face,
I rest on his unchanging grace;
in ev'ry high and stormy gale
my anchor holds within the veil.

[Refrain]
His oath, his covenant, his blood
support me in the whelming flood;
when all around my soul gives way,

he then is all my hope and stay.

[Refrain]
When he shall come with trumpet sound,
O may I then in him be found,
dressed in his righteousness alone,
faultless to stand before the throne"

[Refrain]

Me with Homeowner Ms. Beverly
Photo by Mark Bennett–Tuscaloosa, Alabama–2012

Chapter Four

Fortification

> "The name of the LORD is a strong fortress;
> The godly run to him and are safe."
> Proverbs 18:10 (NLT)

Ms. Beverly leaned her elbows on the porch railing of her new home, nearly finished. In two days, she would be handed the keys and an invoice marked "Paid in Full." A few of us volunteers were listening to her tell her story.

She looked across the street at the concrete slabs—all that remained of some of her neighbors' homes. We knew she was picturing in her mind her neighbors' houses, now gone, and the street as it once was. Just a year before, both sides were lined with a dozen or more ranch-style homes.

Though we were all with her, listening, Ms. Beverly seemed to be talking aloud to herself. She was reliving before, during, and after the EF-4 storm.

There was an older couple that once lived diagonally from her—both the husband and his wife were killed, she said. Another woman up the street was found dead in a field and her badly injured husband in the rubble of their home. Several others lost everything and decided not to return. After seeing the path of destruction and the debarked and leaf-stripped trees, I could understand why.

Ms. Beverly had it mentally recorded inside herself.

Her family was with her in the house when the 190-mph winds hit. Their home didn't have a basement. So, when the storm converged on them and the house began to break apart, the entire family piled atop one another on the couch. Not able to find her father once the tornado passed, Ms. Beverly at first feared she had lost him. He was found alive under some furniture. Fortunately, they all survived.

This family, one of about four on the block, decided to stay and repair or rebuild their home. This time, however, the Beverly home included a safe room.

Safe room in Tuscaloosa, Alabama–2012

The function of a *safe room* is just that—to provide safety and protection.

Ideally, a safe room is built underground, but if that's not possible, anchoring it to a good foundation is necessary. Further protection requires adding reinforced walls and doors, impenetrable against debris and strong winds, a strong door-locking system, and even bullet-proofing materials.[12] The type of safe room needed depends on what it's protecting someone from.

In the Midwest, a safe room is often used to protect families from tornadoes and strong winds. In the Southeast, protection from hurricanes is more in demand. In some areas of the country, as in the West for example, fires occur and spread more quickly than a human can outrun. These are natural disasters that would be a reason for a shelter. Safe rooms are even built to protect from extreme events like home invasions and terrorism. Regardless of the reason, these protective structures are only temporary places of refuge that people hope they will never need to use.

Seeing the physical damage that the tornado did to the town in Alabama and listening to the emotional toll the storm put on its citizens made me understand our real need is *assurance*, not insurance. That in the event of a storm, a person or family wants to believe they have a chance of survival.

I've only experienced a little of what Ms. Beverly went through, but it was enough. I do know what fear of a Midwestern storm is.

In 1993, we had only a few minutes warning that a storm was heading in our direction. Our first home did not have a basement. We went to the closest thing we had to a safe room— the bathroom—and we waited with our two boys. We planned to ride the storm out in the bathtub. But, when a large oak tree in the backyard fell on the house, my husband said, "We have to get out of here!"

We fled in the middle of the storm. Mark grabbed one of the boys, and I scooped up the other. We jumped the chain-link fence and ran in the pelting rain and hail to the neighbors' underground shelter.

It all happened so fast that part of it's a blur. That may be a blessing. When the storm had passed, we and our neighbors exited the shelter—wet, sore, and in shock. Everything was eerily quiet.

The neighborhood was wrecked. Trees and powerlines were down everywhere. Leaves were plastered on cars and houses. Metal debris, roofing, trampolines, and splintered boards littered yards and streets. Most eerie was the silence afterwards. The deafening wind, pounding hail, and downpour of rain all were gone.

The damage to our home was significant, but what the storm did to me psychologically was overwhelming. I struggle to this day with fear and panic whenever a storm warning is declared in the area because of what I saw and heard that day.

Like Ms. Beverly's family, I, too, value assurance that my family is taken care of. I want my family to be safe. That storm created fear and doubt in me. It became a stronghold.

It takes resilience and courage to bounce back from storms in life, and I pray that one day, God gives me so much courage that I fear storms no more. I want to have back what the storm took from me—my peace.

I not only feel weak as a parent and as an adult, but as a believer. I question myself. *Where's your faith? What kind of example are you to the kids?*

Do you ever feel that way? Something comes storming into your life, and you want to run from it? Does it challenge your courage? Your faith? Do you fear a storm in your future?

The apostle Paul tells all of us that in our weakness, God's power is made perfect because His grace is all we need. It is sufficient. Paul goes so far as to celebrate his own weakness because he says weakness allows Christ's strength and power to rest *on us*.

"For when I am weak, then I am strong" (2 Corinthians 12:9-10 NIV). I am still working on my storm fear. I am not strong because of anything I have done, but rather it is Christ's assurance that tells me God is omnipotent and *for me*.

Mark 4:35-41 says when Jesus was sleeping in the boat, the apostles feared the approaching strong storms. Many in the boat were fishermen, so they must have been fully experienced in and aware of storms at sea. The waves and wind had to be so severe that the men truly believed they would perish.

The men feared for their lives. They woke Jesus.

With just a word from Jesus, the seas become still—the winds become calm.

What I need to remember, what you need to know, is Jesus is with the men in the boat. Jesus is in the circumstance, the storm. Jesus isn't afraid. He is with us in our circumstance. He is with us in the storm. Jesus hears us when we call out to Him. He isn't afraid. He calms the storm and his disciples. He can calm our storm and us in our fear.

Yet, like the disciples, I fight my own human nature.

Every building project has its challenges, and I am a project in the works. When my faith is strong, my fears are weak. When my fears are strong, my faith is weak.

What a building is built upon and how it might fare during "storms" in the future determine what the building needs. The tallest building in London, the Shard, is built on soft clay. The Burj Khalifa in Dubai has salty water running underground,[13] and in New York City, the wind could actually bring down several buildings.[14]

"Foundations are vital to anchor buildings but [truth be told,] many skyscrapers around the world are not on solid ground,"[15] according to Samsung C&T, an engineering and construction trade publication. For every challenge or weakness, a solution must be found.

That, I believe, is where our weaknesses lie. We lack solid ground. I lack solid ground...unless I have Christ with me.

I have seen the damage and power of storms, and I know I cannot stop them. So, what do I do? I flee—to whatever I can for shelter. I was putting greater faith in my basement, bathroom tub, and neighbors' storm shelter in that moment than I was in the Lord—and that's when fear robbed me of my peace.

When I, when *we*, fall into that thinking, we need to say to ourselves, reminding ourselves over and over, that Jesus says, "Peace I leave with you; *my* peace I give you. I do not give you as the world gives you. Do not let your hearts be troubled and do not be afraid" (John 14:27 NIV).

Shalom is **God's** peace, not the world's peace. The world can't offer us that. God's shalom is unmatchable.

A foundation can shift because of strong winds, but there are ways to protect what's built upon that foundation from collapsing. One way is to build a strong middle, or core.

When a storm arises, weather experts tell people to go to the center-most room in the building. That is the strongest, most reinforced place to flee. Everything else may be torn away, but after the storm, the core area is more likely to be standing.

The heart and mind and soul are the core for human beings and believers. These are the most valuable parts of who we are.

"Above all else, guard your heart, for everything you do flows from it" (Proverbs 4:23 NIV). Other versions of the Bible, substitute *heart* for *thoughts*. We must do all we can to protect both because they are our refuge.

First, we need to take those thoughts captive immediately when our fear grabs hold of us, like my fear of storms does me. We need to recognize where fear is leading our mind and stop it right there. Don't let it go any farther.

Second, we need to guard our heart and thoughts by learning what is good and what is evil (Psalm 119:11). When we know God's Word and ways, we can recognize his hand in our lives, and we won't be fooled by thunder or a few dark clouds. *Training ourselves* means letting Scripture guide us, rather than believing just anything we hear or think we see.

Third, we can protect our heart and mind by praying. We must choose what we let our mind think about. My imagination is a blessing and a curse at times. I let my mind take me off in directions that help me teach and write and draw, which is such a blessing. Other times, my imagination sends me in directions that get me anxious, panicky, and sometimes, inconsolable. At that point, it's difficult for me to set my feelings aside and lasso my thoughts. I know where my fear of storms is from—my experiences and my imagination.

It helps me greatly to crank up the music in my car or house and sing worship songs. I also take my thoughts captive by drawing or writing. These both change the direction of my thinking.

The apostle Paul encourages us to not only redirect our thoughts but also our living. Paul writes, "I urge you to live a life worthy of the calling you have received" (Eph. 4:1 NIV).

What would that look like? A life worthy of your calling? Jesus' life and teaching are our model. That's our goal. The closer we get to Him, the more we will resemble Him.

The *best* way to guard our mind and heart is to turn ourselves over to the Lord, to put upon Him what we do and let Him establish our steps. Remember? To *commit* all we do to the Lord. When we accept Christ, the Holy Spirit indwells us. He will never leave nor abandon us. The Spirit can search us—search our heart and our thoughts—and He can "create in us a clean heart" and direct our steps.

The Lord offers to be our safe room, our refuge. He can protect our mind and heart, calm us in the strongest storms, rebuild us better than we were before, and block anything that comes to steal, kill, or destroy us.

Think. In a situation, we may need a way out. We practice drills as small children in school. Flight attendants tell us what to do in case of an emergency evacuation. We can't stop the storms, but we can flee or shelter ourselves from it.

Often, God gives us a way out of our situation.

Our debt of sin is marked "Paid in Full" when we accept his gifts, and He hands us the key that opens the door to salvation.

We shouldn't live in fear when we can live in a strong fortress, be safely protected, and flee trouble when it comes our way. That assurance is God's love and grace.

I invite you to join me in this prayer:

ord Jesus, You yourself were human. Agonizing over the plan God had for you at the cross, you sweat blood. Yet, your heart and mind were steadfast. You went to the Father in prayer. You endured pain none of us could bear. Yet, You stayed the course. You faced death and won!

Open my eyes and ears, Lord, to the tricks of the enemy and remove my fear. Help me keep my heart and mind away from the enemy's vices. Let me bury myself in your protective arms and find peace and safety there. Amen

Application: A Fortress for My Soul

The word *fortress* is often considered synonymous with *fort*, but actually there are differences. A fort's main purpose is military protection. It's beneficial in war. A fortress, however, can be a large fort, multiple forts, or be an entire town—strongly fortified, of course. It is built to protect *everything* within its walls from attack, not just military troops.[16] Therefore, a fort can be a fortress, but a fortress is not always a fort.

A safe room in a home would be considered more of a fort and the entire house a fortress. A house may have a fenced yard, locks and alarms, doors and windows. A house may contain many rooms. However, if a storm hits that particular house, it's quite possible the doors, windows, entire rooms, and outer walls could peel away in the winds. However, a fort, or safe room, is built to withstand those winds. People in other rooms of the house during a severe storm could be injured or killed. Those in the safe room are "fortified" and more likely to survive.

I've seen a safe room being built. It is made before outer walls, internal framing, or trusses are set. Safe rooms have thick cinder-block walls, with concrete poured in the blocks and metal straps are used for reinforcement. The specialized door to the safe room can take a powerful blow from flying debris and not easily be penetrated. Safe rooms cost a great deal, but they are assurance that you and your family may make it through a storm.

Who among us hasn't witnessed the power of a storm—either through personal experience or through media coverage? When a weather warning sounds, do we not think of grabbing the things most precious to us and fleeing to a safe place—a refuge?

Name what (or who) we anchor or fasten down for protection.

1. (i.e. our children in car seats) _____
2. _____
3. _____
4. _____
5. _____

Name careers where "protection" is their primary responsibility.

1. (i.e. policemen) _____
2. _____
3. _____
4. _____
5. _____

In Psalm 18:1-2 (NLT), David sings a song of praise, having been saved by the Lord from a different kind of storm—an attack by Saul and his enemies. "I love you, LORD; you are my strength. The LORD is my rock, my fortress, and my savior." David says God is his rock, or safe room, where David finds protection.

What is one *storm* you have experienced that you feared you might not survive? (i.e. health issues, finances, relationships, employment, prejudices, oppression, weather storm, etc.)

_____
_____

What thoughts or fears ran through your mind or in your heart at that time?

_____
_____

To whom or what did you turn during the storm for protection?

_____

The prophet Isaiah says the Lord is "a refuge for **the poor**, a refuge for **the needy** in **their** distress, a shelter from the storm and a shade from the heat. For the breath of the ruthless is like a storm driving [**me**] against a wall" (Isaiah 25:4 NLT).

Rewrite Isaiah 25:4, inputting **your name** where the bold italics is above.

The Lord is

_____

_____

_____

_____

_____

Who else do you know could use such encouragement in their own struggles and storms?

_____   _____

_____   _____

Listen to Casting Crowns' song "Just Be Held."[12]

Remember, when you can't take your eyes off of the storm, you may even wonder if God loves you at all. But, take your thoughts captive, and "just be held." Remember too, that He is on his throne and He has not forgotten you. Everything is falling into place.

Call out to Jesus. *Commit* to him your greatest fears, and He will establish your safe place.

Construction of One World Trade Center, New York City–2011

Chapter Five

Stress Test

⋙⋅—•—⋅❖⋅—•—⋅⋘

"But if we look forward to something we don't yet have,
we must wait patiently and confidently."
Romans 8:25 (NLT)

"*H*ow long before it's dry?"

The contractor who just poured your basketball court may answer and correct you in the same breath.

To a contractor, concrete doesn't dry. It *cures*. It's the time concrete takes to strengthen.

After only one day, concrete can handle weight without leaving an imprint. The truth is, however, concrete never fully stops curing. As long as the cement is in contact with moisture, the ingredients continue to bond, and it continues to strengthen.[18]

What's the ultimate goal? A strong and durable finished product.

Strength and *durability* are not the same. Something that is strong isn't necessarily durable, and something durable isn't always strong. A powerful shot putter may throw a 16-pound iron shot more than 60 feet, but he may not outlast other smaller team members running around the track. And, a palm tree may not be as strong as an oak tree, but it's able to bend and withstand hours of tropical winds, without breaking. It's more durable.

Strength enables something, or someone, to handle a great weight or intense pressure. Whereas, *durability* makes something last longer without falling apart.

How does a contractor know if his concrete is as strong as he needs it to be? And, how does he know if it is durable? He tests it.

God wants his people to be strong and durable finished products as well. Throughout Scripture, we read where many He chooses are tested.

Moses, Job, Daniel, and David, for example, all bear the weight of their own burdens while some carry the heft of an entire nation. Either way, those who turn to the Lord in their battles and are faithful are given incredible strength, but those who follow their own desires and are disobedient are weakened and defeated. One such person is Samson, the Nazarite.

Physically, Samson is stronger than any man or army that he meets. Before he was born, Samson's parents vowed to the Lord that the son they had waited so long to have would serve God his whole life. The Lord gives Samson unmatchable physical strength that becomes a tool in God's hands. However, Samson isn't always obedient to his parents or God, and eventually God allows that strength to be taken away—temporarily anyway.

Samson's faith, not his muscles, is tested. After revealing to the beautiful, Philistine woman Delilah where his strength comes from (his uncut hair), Samson is lulled to sleep. Seven locks of his hair are cut, and just like that, his strength is gone. With the aid of Delilah, the Philistines take the weakened Samson captive and blind him.

It's then, Samson turns back to the Lord. This Nazarite asks for strength one last time.

"Sovereign Lord, remember me again. O God, please strengthen me just one more time," Samson prays (Judges 16:28 NLT).

Why does he ask to be strong again, even if just once?

Samson wants to serve the Lord and the Lord's people, as his parents had promised he would. Samson acknowledges his disobedience and repents.

When the moment comes, Samson is given incredible strength that he uses to bring the entire temple down on top of the Philistine rulers and all of those inside—Samson included. All are killed (Judges 13-16).

To test concrete's strength, it's usually exposed to great pressure, to determine its breaking point.[12]

With God, Samson's strength has no breaking point. *Without* God, he is a man who can easily be defeated. Samson's restored strength comes from his obedient and faithful heart.

How much stress can we handle before we break? Do we remain obedient and faithful *in the middle* of the struggle?

Throughout the Bible, God tells us to fear not. He is with us and will strengthen us. The Lord tells us He will uphold us with his righteous right hand (Isaiah 41:10). Jesus himself says that we will have many trials and sorrows here on earth, but He has overcome the world (John 16:33). I Peter 5:7 says we can cast all our anxieties upon the Lord.

Our help and *strength* come from the Lord. Like David, Job, Daniel, and Moses, we too have the power within us to part seas, move mountains, defeat lions, and fall giants; like Jesus, we have the ability to feed nations, heal the hurting, and endure persecution. Our power is the Holy Spirit and the gifts He gives us.

When our boys were young, we often bought them Plain Pocket Jeans from JCPenney. Why? Because the fabric seemed indestructible. Skateboarding and bicycle falls, sliding into base, and crawling around on the carpet didn't easily destroy the knees or rear end of this particular brand of jeans. After seeing what these two kids could do to other brands, my husband and I learned which jeans would last longest.

When these same boys and their sister became teenagers, it was time to put them in cars of their own. We searched for vehicles that would last through high school and hopefully college, as well as protect them and take a beating. A full-sized pickup truck and a Jeep Grand Cherokee both proved to be very durable.

Durability is different from strength, and testing durability is different as well.

It's crucial that concrete used in bridges or skyscrapers, for example, lasts longer than the concrete of a residential driveway. Thousands and maybe millions of people's lives rely on the integrity and longevity of a specific building's materials. Truth is, not all concrete is the same. Some mixtures break down and come apart more easily than others while others are as strong as steel.

In the book of Genesis, Jacob's son Joseph is continually tested, yet this young man continually resists the influences around him—his brothers, Potiphar's wife, prison inmates, and Egypt's Pharaoh himself. Joseph perseveres and proves himself resilient. He shows integrity despite adversity. His faith makes him durable.

Joseph lives to be 110 years old. Of those years, a great number are spent in service to others. His ability to persevere while enslaved, to be resilient while in prison, and to resist temptation and the desire to seek revenge, all show a man who serves God's purpose while remaining faithful (Genesis 37-50).

Samson and Joseph are not alone in possessing such strength and durability. We, too, can pass the tests of stress and time. Be assured, we all will be tested, and the weight we carry at times may seem unbearable. These seasons can also seem endless. However, it's in those times God can feel closest to us and make the most change in us.

"[After] you have suffered a little while, he will restore, support, and strengthen you, and he will place you on a firm foundation" (I Peter 5:10 NLT).

Peter tells us God will restore us from our suffering and bring us to spiritual health—taking away the weight that oppresses us and placing it upon himself. God will place us on the "firm foundation" of Christ, and then, on Christ, we are built.

Strength is revealed *in the battle*, and durability *in the war*. It is God's will that we be made strong and durable through faith.

The Burj Khalifa, a 160-story skyscraper in the United Arab Emirates, truly is a wonder. This record-breaking structure took six years and more than 12,000 construction workers to build.[20]

From the ground up, every conceivable obstacle and adverse condition had to be considered. It has to be strong and durable. Has. to. be.

One of the first challenges to building this one-half-mile tall skyscraper that could house 35,000 people at one time is the complication lurking underground.[21]

As earlier mentioned, at the root of the Burj Khalifa is salty underground water, eight times saltier than seawater. This salt is extremely corrosive and would be dangerous to the weight-bearing steel embedded in the foundation. This salt would eat away at the strength of the steel. To protect the steel, building contractors added a metal substitute to the concrete mixture. If the salt attacks anything in the concrete, it will be this added substitute.[22]

If we accept Jesus Christ as our Lord and Savior, He offers himself as our substitute. Jesus will fight against forces that try to steal our strength and can knock us down. Satan's nature strives to make us feel weak and defeated. If we fail, he hopes we take others down with us. He doesn't want us to reach out to God for support.

However, as believers, we have the strength and power of the Lord within us—the risen Lord—who has already defeated the enemy at the cross.

The builders of the Burj Khalifa also knew that safely evacuating or rescuing 35,000 people from 160 floors is an impossibility. September 11, 2001, taught builders that anyone and anything can be the target of an attack. Therefore, the design of the Burj Khalifa (two times the size of the World Trade Towers) includes nine refuge rooms (like safe rooms)—built every 30 floors—offering protection from smoke and fire to those who can reach the shelter. Contractors hoped to make a strong and durable place for people to go until the building is safe or the people can be rescued. Strong and durable. That's what these refuge rooms in the Burj Khalifa are designed to be.[23]

Designers, architects, and builders can pour all their knowledge and resources into creating something as magnificent or greater than the Burj Khalifa. But, no foundation has been, is, or ever will be stronger than Jesus Christ. No cornerstone is as true as Jesus Christ. No refuge or fortress stronger than the Father. No pillar mightier than our God in Heaven. There is no temple like Jesus Christ—who could be torn down and three days later be rebuilt. Jesus, our Redeemer, who promised his disciples that

He would be leaving them, told them to trust God and trust in Jesus. He was going away to "prepare a place" in his Father's home for all of his children (John 14:1-3 NLT).

Believe this: Pouring in all his wisdom and all his power, God designed you, and you are truly magnificent. You are His masterpiece. You are the dwelling place of the Holy Spirit. You can stand tall with the strength and durability that come from the Spirit dwelling inside of you.

I say again, We *are* God's house, if we keep our courage, and remain confident in our hope in Christ (Hebrews 3:6 NLT). Courage, confidence, and hope. Add to those now *strength* and *durability*. All are ours when we are built *on* Christ and *in* Him.

I invite you to listen to the song "Stay Strong" by Danny Gokey.[24] Reflect for a while on how God has made you stronger over time.

James, the half-brother of Jesus, writes:

"Consider it a sheer gift, friends, when tests and challenges come at you from all sides. You know that under pressure, your faith-life is forced into the open and shows its true colors. So don't try to get out of anything prematurely. Let it do its work so you become mature and well-developed, not deficient in any way" (James 1:2-4 MSG).

It's time to add *strong* and *durable* to the words you would use to describe yourself as a believer in Christ.

Application:
Weighed Down and Worn Out

Our *strength* is often tested when we are challenged to lift, carry, push, or pull weight to which we aren't accustomed. Students start back to school lugging heavy backpacks. Grandparents, carrying their grandchildren around for very long, will feel it the next day. Some challenges, like moving furniture, are more than we can manage alone. Not all weighty burdens are measured in pounds, however. Some make our heart and mind feel heavy.

Where in life do you feel a lack of *strength*—physically, mentally, or spiritually?

Make a list of responsibilities, debts, commitments, obligations, etc. that weigh heavily upon your heart, mind, or soul.

_____	_____
_____	_____
_____	_____
_____	_____
_____	_____

Are any of those ones you've endured for *a long time*?

Circle any of those that you listed above that God is not strong enough to carry or willing to walk through with you—even if it's a long walk.

You didn't need to pick up your pen there, did you? There is **nothing** God cannot or would not carry for you. He is with you.

Psalm 145:14 says, "The LORD upholds **all** who are falling and raises up **all** who are bowed down" (my emphasis, ESV).

The Psalm says, the Lord "upholds all" and "raises up all." God's love and strength never wear out and never run out. When we call upon Him to lift from us our worries and burdens or see us through till our struggle is over, He promises to give us rest.

Test Him in this.
Take Him at his word.
Let Him take control.

When we let ourselves be yoked to him, He will show us a better, "lighter" way.

I invite you to join me in this prayer:

Father God, When I feel I am letting my thoughts rob me of my strength and shake my confidence, take back that power I've given to other people or to the enemy. I hand myself and my circumstances over to you, Lord. I pray for patience—patience that I should extend to others—the same patience that you, God, have for me. I pray for you to help me, Lord, with my responsibilities, debts, commitments, and obligations, particularly (.....). Deliver me from and through whatever you choose, Lord. I surrender the weight of my worries to you.

In Jesus Christ's name, Amen

Our home in Prairieton, Indiana–2016
A header was installed to maintain support

Chapter Six

Razing Walls, Raising Walls

"I devoted myself to the work on this wall."
Nehemiah 5:16 (NIV)

*O*ur contractor said the wall was a load-bearing wall. He couldn't just take it out. He had to insert large beams for the wall to continue supporting the house. Modifications had to be made.

Walls go up and walls come down. Sometimes, it's planned, and other times it's out of our control. Why walls are needed at all varies. Some are meant to separate and divide, and others are essential for support. Walls may be for protection, and other times, they create boundaries or a beautiful appearance.

Whatever the purpose, walls exist in all of our lives. They exist in our homes, workplaces, along the highway, between countries, and in our relationships. Some walls can last, and others are temporary. Truth is, some walls God wants for us, and some He doesn't.

Throughout the Bible, walls were more than just details mentioned. Some were obstacles that had to be removed, and others needed to be built. Some were built by men. Others by

God. Regardless, big or little, walls can separate us from God or be a tool in his hand. They can symbolize his strength or reflect our obedience (or disobedience).

One wall that was a tool in God's hand is found in the book of Daniel. In Chapter 5, God uses the wall of Belshazzar's banquet hall in the king's palace as a slate to relay a message to the Babylonian king. Belshazzar doesn't learn the lesson from the mistakes of his father, who took glory away from God and elevated himself and other gods. Belshazzar lets his wives, nobles, and concubines drink from goblets his father's army has taken from the Temple in Jerusalem.

A hand appears during the banquet, and a finger writes on the wall "Mene, Mene, Tekel, Parsin," words only Daniel can understand. Daniel explains first that Belshazzar has set himself up against God in heaven, and the hand has been sent by God, who "holds in his hand your life and all your ways" (Verse 23 NIV).

Daniel reveals that the message tells Belshazzar and all at the banquet that the king is about to die, he has failed as a leader, and his kingdom is about to be conquered. That very night, all that was written on the wall occurred.

This is a time that God uses a wall to deliver a message. He reveals his power and intolerance for rulers who govern with pride and lead their people away from God.

God doesn't just *use* walls, He puts them in place. When God made Adam, God wanted to be close to the one He created in His image. Adam takes walks with God in the garden. God provides for Adam's every need, including making him a mate. Adam and Eve tend the garden and have full liberties there, except one–don't eat from the Tree of Knowledge of Good and Evil. God doesn't put a wall around the Tree. He gives

Adam (and Eve) the choice-the free will-to make decisions. There are no barriers between God and man, just an expectation. However, when both Adam and Eve decide to eat from the forbidden tree-against God's command-they separate themselves from God. Adam has never experienced shame before and never hidden from the Father.

God confronts both Adam and Eve for their disobedience and tells them each the consequences of their actions. In God's final words to Adam and Eve, He separates himself from them and all to follow. He creates a "wall."

At the entrance to the garden, God places mighty cherubim to the east of the Garden of Eden. And he places a flaming sword that flashes back and forth to guard the way to the tree of life (Genesis 3:24). Man and God are now physically separated. Adam and Eve will now struggle in a world wrought with sin, and one day, they both will die. The "wall" God puts between Adam and Eve not only separates them from God but also from the Tree of Life-that forever would have provided for them.

It isn't until the death, burial, and resurrection of Jesus that the wall separating us from God is removed, and we can forever spend our days on earth and our eternity with the Father—if we accept Jesus as our Lord and Savior.

Remember, walls go up and they also come down. God can show his strength and power by putting a wall in place or bringing one down. He can do it himself or empower us with nothing more than trumpets sounding and army shouts, as in the case of Joshua and his army.

After 40 years of wandering the desert, the people of Israel are no longer slaves in Egypt and are soon to reach the Promised Land. Moses and Aaron are dead, and Joshua is now leading

God's people. One of the first obstacles the Lord will have them face is the city of Jericho.

To appreciate the magnitude of what God does in Jericho, we must know the incredible challenge this fortified city is. Jericho has two walls surrounding it entirely. The inner wall towers 46 feet above ground level, and the outer wall stands 30-40 feet tall, if its retaining wall is counted. Between the two walls is a slanted embankment with a great amount of area. There, the poor build their houses and those seeking refuge take shelter. Joshua and his people will have to get past two enormous walls, approximately six feet thick and well protected, to conquer Jericho.[25]

God instructs Joshua to march his priests and army around the outer walls of the city–once daily for six days in a row. Joshua does just as he is told. Hearing only the Israelite priests blowing their horns, Jericho knows the Israelites are there. But, with a city well fortified and supplied with food and water, the people of Jericho may not be as concerned as they should be.[26]

On the seventh day, Joshua and his men march around the city seven times. At his command, his people all shout at once, and the walls come down–both of them–and the Israelites take the city of Jericho.

"When the [Israelite] people heard the sound of the ram's horns, they shouted [as God had instructed] as loud as they could. Suddenly, the walls of Jericho collapsed, and the Israelites charged straight into the town and captured it" (Joshua 6:20 NLT).

Archaeologists agree. The walls of Jericho collapsed. But, some argued evidence didn't support that it could have been the time period of the Israelite attack...until Dr. Bryant Wood, American Biblical archaeologist, re-examined the fallen walls and charred contents of the city.

Dr. Wood found the fallen walls not only created an opening into the city but made it possible for the Israelite "army to go up, and everyone straight in" (Joshua 6:5). Dr. Wood said both walls came *crumbling* down creating "ramps" so the people of Israel were easily able to invade.[27] In Joshua 6:5, God tells what He *will* do and fifteen verses later, it happens. "[So] everyone charged straight in, and they took the city" (Joshua 6:20 NIV). The people of Israel take the city of Jericho and bring down its walls because it is God's will, and they are obedient to the Father.

God powerfully takes down probably one of the most impenetrable walls man could build, and yet God puts a "wall of protection" around Rahab and her family who lived in Jericho. Joshua had promised her that she and her family would be spared.

Archaeologists argue that it was likely an earthquake that brought the walls of Jericho down. Still, if God wanted to use an earthquake or horns and shouts, either way, God provided a way for the obstacle of Jericho to be removed and for God himself to be glorified. Dr. Bryant Wood states, "If God did use an earthquake to accomplish His purposes that day, it was still a miracle since it happened at precisely the right moment, and was manifested in such a way as to protect Rahab's house. No matter what agency God used, it was ultimately He who, through the faith of the Israelites, brought the walls down."[28]

Dr. Wood writes, "Jericho is a wonderful spiritual lesson for God's people yet today. There are times when we find ourselves facing enormous 'walls' that are impossible to break down by human strength. If we put our faith in God and follow his commandments, He will perform 'great and mighty things' and give us the victory."[29]

Since the fall of Adam, people have been building walls to shelter themselves from the weather, to protect their assets, and to keep out their enemies. Just know, if God builds a wall, it is impenetrable. But, if He wants a wall to come down, nothing and no one can hold back His might. The wall will come down.

Throughout the Bible, God's "walls" are not always made of brick and mortar. They come in many forms:

- (Exodus 14:21-22 NIV) "...the LORD drove the sea back with a strong east wind and turned it into dry land. The waters were divided, and the Israelites went through the sea on dry ground, with a **wall of water** on their right and on their left."
- (Psalm 121:5-6 NIV) "...The LORD watches over you— the LORD is **your shade** at your right hand; the sun will not harm you by day, nor the moon by night."
- (Isaiah 5:5 NIV) "I will remove its **hedge** and it will be consumed; I will break down its wall and it will become trampled ground."
- (Zechariah 2:4-5 NIV) "Run, tell that young man, 'Jerusalem will be a city without walls because of the great number of people and animals in it. And I myself will be **a wall of fire** around it,' declares the LORD, 'and I will be its glory within.'"
- (Psalm 3:3 NIV) "But you, LORD, are **a shield around me**, my glory, the One who lifts my head high."
- (Psalm 57:1 NIV) "...my God, have mercy on me, for in you I take refuge. I will take refuge **in the shadow of your wings** until the disaster has passed."

- (Psalm 125:2 NIV) "**As the mountains** surround Jerusalem, so the LORD surrounds his people both now and forevermore."

God's protection and his refuge come in many ways. Sometimes, however, He allows us to fall to our enemies because of our disobedience, someone else's disobedience, or a greater purpose we may not understand.

At the mention of September 11, we usually generate shocking images of planes crashing into the buildings, towers collapsing, and a gaping hole in the Pentagon exterior. Then, the question "Why?" Why would anybody want to hurt so many people? Why would God let this happen and not stop it? Why would a loving God allow this?

Those walls came down as the result of sin in this world. The minute Adam and Eve broke the one commandment God gave them, that introduced sin and death into the world. God didn't stop Adam or Eve. Remember He gave them free will to decide if they were going to obey or not, just as He has given us free will. God watches every day as sin manifests in people in the form of illness, suffering, lust, jealousy, anger, and hate. Our pain breaks His heart just as it did September 11. The terrorists who took over those planes and drove them into the towers chose their actions. There was sin in the hearts of those men.

God knows what is in our heart. Our intentions and thoughts are led by it. In the story of Nehemiah, God softens the heart of a king to help a faithful servant Nehemiah build a wall for his God and God's people. Rebuilding this wall reflects Nehemiah's faithfulness to his God and his people.

Nehemiah, cupbearer to Persia's king Artaxerxes, resides many miles away from his people living in Judah. Though his service is to a foreign king, his heart is with God's people, especially in Jerusalem. God's remnant people, who have returned from Babylonian exile, are on Nehemiah's mind. When he learns from his brother that "the wall of Jerusalem is broken down, and its gates have been burned with fire," he weeps and prays and fasts that God's favor be upon his people once again (Nehemiah 1:3-11).

King Artaxerxes recognizes his servant Nehemiah's unusual melancholy and says, "This can be nothing but sadness of the heart" (Nehemiah 2:2 NIV).

"What is it you want?" Artaxerxes asks Nehemiah.

Nehemiah prays first and then answers the king. Nehemiah asks if he can return to the city in Judah to help rebuild it. God not only shows Nehemiah favor through Artaxerxes agreement, but he also is given God's favor through safe travel, building materials for the wall and gates, and protection.

It doesn't take the people of Jerusalem long to see that Nehemiah brings with him God's favor, and the city and its people no longer feel disgrace.

"They replied, 'Let us start rebuilding.' So they began this good work" (Nehemiah 2:18 NIV).

In spite of being scoffed at and threatened, Nehemiah and the people of Judah "worked early and late, from sunrise to sunset." They work with one hand and are ready to fight any adversaries with the other (Nehemiah 4:17-21 NLT).

Half of the wall goes up quickly because the Bible says "the people had worked with enthusiasm" (Nehemiah 4:6 NLT).

It takes only 52 days for the entire wall around Jerusalem to be rebuilt–in spite of the threats, distractions, accusations, and intimidation. In fact, Nehemiah pushes back enemy accusations and calls them lies. Nehemiah becomes all the more determined and when his enemies see the wall is completed, "they realized this work had been done with the help of our God" (Nehemiah 6:16 NIV).

Before you build a wall in a relationship, in your thoughts, or in your decisions, ask the Father what his will is for you. In *Discerning the Voice of God,* author and speaker Priscilla Shirer says, "If you're currently struggling with a decision, confused as to whether the voice you're hearing is coming from the Spirit of Truth or not, ask yourself...

- 'Will it contradict the truth found in Scripture?
- 'Will it cause me to indulge in sin of any kind?
- 'Will it encourage me to hypocritically cover up my sin?
- 'Will it give glory to God by magnifying his truth to the people involved?'" (136)[30]

I have many times used and shared Priscilla Shirer's *test* to discern if a decision is from the Father. I add to her thoughts that if a spiritually-mature person affirms the decision, I feel more assured. I stress I turn to someone who has a relationship with Jesus and follows Him to see their thoughts.

We are the tools in God's hand. When we are faithful and serve Him as Nehemiah does, we can be confident and courageous because God is our sword and our shield. And, not only can what seems impossible be accomplished in our lives, God can be glorified by our faithfulness, obedience, and sacrifice. God doesn't need a wall to protect a city, but He does love our putting Him first, above ourselves and all others, and He will help us build up or tear down any wall or barrier He wills for our life...if we ask Him.

I invite you to join me in this prayer:

Heavenly Father, I often pray for a hedge of protection around my family and myself. I know if you build a wall, my enemies cannot reach me, no matter what they try. I have never worried at night if the walls of my home would still be standing in the morning, but many in this world do. Every day. Some may lose their protective walls to eviction, natural disaster, war, or broken relationships. I pray you put all of these families, children, and homeless people in your protective arms and give them peace. Bring faithful servants into the lives of troubled people to connect them to You and Your warm embrace. Amen

Application: Being a Grateful Child

Honestly, I thought I was being punked. I stepped out into the hallway. "What did you say, Mari?"

I wasn't sure I heard my daughter correctly.

She was sitting alone in the kitchen and looking at her phone. She repeated more loudly, "Thanks for having rules for us."

I paused. *Did my fifteen-year-old just thank me for our family rules? Where was this coming from?* I wondered.

"Uh, what do you mean?" I asked.

I walked in the kitchen. Our daughter said she was thankful that her dad and I had the rule for her that she couldn't date until she was sixteen. She explained how it was easier for her to tell her friends, in particular boys, that she had to wait to date. She felt relieved using that as an excuse from doing some of the things her peers were doing. The rule we had in place made her feel safe.

We always told our kids they could use us as scapegoats for saying **no** or **I can't** to their friends. I would happily take the fall for being an uncool, overly-protective parent than see one of my kids get hurt.

God has given us "walls" or boundaries, too. Our heavenly Father is an overly-protective parent who wants to be our scapegoat. In fact, He already has been. If we follow what the Lord God expects of us, we will not only be thankful for the pain He spares us from, but also we, as parents, can show our children what our Father God wants for us as His children.

Thank you, God, for your commandments that keep me safe.

Looking back, there have been times in my adult life that I wish I had respected the "walls" or boundaries better. I could have avoided hurting others and letting people or things into my life that weren't good for me.

Had I stayed within the boundaries, I could have avoided wrecklessly using credit cards, watching movies that weren't good for my mind or spirit, and befriending people who had a negative influence on my attitude and words. Life without boundaries allows the enemy to walk right in. Satan wants to steal, kill, and destroy, and without "walls," we make it that much easier for him.

Again, thank you, God, for your commandments that keep me safe.

Devoting time to reading my Bible and consulting strong Christian mentors have given me accountability and a barometer for how I am living. If I tell myself I can do this on my own and that I know what is best for me, I know I will eventually begin listening to the voices I *want* to hear, not the One I need to hear.

Read Psalm 16. I prefer *The Message* version.

David says in this Psalm that he trusts the Lord to protect him, and rejoices that he has God followers all around him that can counsel him as well. Like David, the Lord has put boundaries on us, and David says, "my choice is you, God, you are first and only." So, no other gods have influence on David. David's heart is happy–on the inside and out–and he is never letting go.

Who in your youth set the rules that you were expected to follow?

_____

Can you name anyone, while you were growing up, who could do whatever they wanted?

_____

On the other hand, did you know anyone who had very strict parents?

_____

King Solomon spoke to parents, "Train up a child in the way he should go; and even when he is old he will not depart from it" (Proverbs 22:6 NIV). Being consistent as a parent helps children understand expectations for them. If a parent makes a point not to curse, steal, bully, or gossip, he can influence his children not to do it either. This lesson will be something children carry with them the rest of their lives. Those are protective walls that we can teach our kids are for their good.

And, what happens when we fail as a child if we cross the line? Correction.

"For the moment all discipline seems painful rather than pleasant, but later it yields the peaceful fruit of righteousness to those who have been trained by it" (Hebrew 12:11 ESV).

How my parents disciplined my sisters and me depended on our age and the offense. Regardless, there were consequences. Often, we were expected to apologize to each other if we were fighting or hurting one another. We might still be angry, but we apologized and eventually moved on.

Too many times walls are built between parents and their children, between husbands and wives, between friends and neighbors because someone won't forgive. This may be a wall that God does not want in your life.

Listen to "Jericho" by Andrew Ripp.[31]

- Where might you have put a wall between you and someone else?

_____

- Is there a wall because of unforgiveness? If it is, is it your unforgiveness or the other person's?

_____

- If you are unsure, pray about it. Ask God to reveal if you have built that wall or if He has. A wall built by God may be a protective Fatherly boundary for your good. A wall built by you may be built from pride or anger which does not please our Father in heaven.

- Do you have a wall between you and the Father? Where might you be shutting Him off from some area of your life?

_____

Photo by Mark Bennett

Chapter Seven

The Power Source

"Separated, you can't produce a thing."
John 15:5-6 (MSG)

*O*ur Mercury Comet was nearly restored. Paint job and striping, engine repairs, upholstery, and carpeting. All done. The last touch to the four-year project was to add a radio.

Unfortunately, one screw, just one, driven into a wire behind the radio, fried the car's entire wiring system. Nothing, *nothing!* electrical worked. Our mechanic said that we had to find a wiring harness for our 40-year-old car.

"You're kidding me, right?"

He wasn't.

Most parts and accessories that we had already found were from a salvage yard in rural Illinois. Aside from pulling some bumper parts earlier, nothing had been as complicated as stripping a wiring harness from a scrapped, tireless car embedded six inches in the hardened ground.

Challenge accepted.

Not only did we successfully remove a harness from under the dash, but we also removed all of the wires that ran to it–from the very front of the car to the very back.

When we walked into the mechanic's shop with the part and its wires, he was astounded.

Momentarily, we felt quite proud until our guy said he next needed the wiring schematics to do the job. He needed to see how the car was originally designed to make the harness communicate and relay power to the other parts of the car.

Two months later, the car was finished.

Power is essential. Think of the wiring inside of our house walls. Now, think on a much larger scale, like a skyscraper. In some ways, they and the wiring harness have a similar function. Power needs to be received and dispersed safely. To get lighting, communication signals, data, and HVAC (Heating, Ventilation, Air Conditioning) to do what they were designed to do, power needs to reach each part. Like electrical panels of a house or electrical-service rooms of a skyscraper, that wiring harness houses power and communicates with the different systems and mechanisms we want and need.

Jesus tells us in John 15 how separate from Him we are nothing, but connected to Him, Jesus will hear us and act. The power of Jesus is ours to utilize.

The Message version puts it this way:

"I am the Vine, you are the branches. When you're joined with me and I with you, the relation intimate and organic, the harvest is sure to be abundant. **Separated, you can't produce a thing.** Anyone who separates from me is deadwood, gathered up and thrown on the bonfire. But if you make yourselves at home with me and my words are at home in you, you can be sure that **whatever you ask will be listened to and acted upon.** This is how my Father shows who he is—when you produce grapes, when you mature as my disciples." (Verses 5-8)

Jesus is the Vine. That's where power is. The power that feeds everything. We believers are the branches. When we connect to Him and He to us, God's will is accomplished (Verses 1-3). Jesus tells us that we will be fruitful as his disciples because of our connectedness to Him. However, when we don't connect with Jesus, we "can't produce a thing." In fact, Jesus says God will cut himself off from us, like a farmer prunes fruitless branches because God looks at us as disconnected "deadwood."

An electrician would remove any unused or stray wires by "pruning" them as well. If there's no power service running in them or they aren't being used, they certainly serve no purpose.

Communication is essential when working with power. Mark Bendix, writing for *Consulting-Specifying Engineer,* states many hands go into putting a building together safely. Structural engineers must communicate with electrical engineers, and architects must work closely with electrical engineers. All have to communicate with the building owner, the builder, and the local electric and water companies to discuss costs, complications, and utility compliance.[32] Professionals from many different fields are needed to pool their experience and expertise, and yet sometimes…things still go wrong.

It takes many hands to produce a car. Communication among designers, engineers, manufacturers, and even mechanics make and keep an automobile running, yet recalls and system failures happen.

On the contrary, we were created as God said, in the image of the Father, Son, and Holy Spirit (Genesis 1: 26). The perfect blueprint. We exist because He exists.

Every cell, every tissue, every organ, and every system of our body is engineered and made by God, the sole architect and creator.

God wired us as living, breathing human beings. King David talks about how God put all of our complex systems together before we were born.

In Psalm 139:13, David says God formed our inward parts and knitted us together in our mother's womb. Our heart, lungs, stomach, brain…all of these organs are building blocks–parts of our cardiovascular, respiratory, digestive, and central nervous systems.

Physically, we are a single structure, but our body is made up of cells, tissues, organs and systems. Each organ with a particular function and each system connect these organs to work together. God has orchestrated every cell to come together to give us the body or system that we have.

"[Survival] of the body depends on the body's maintaining or restoring…its internal environment."[33]

Specialists from all over the world can try to help us maintain and restore our cars, our homes, and our bodies. However, there are limitations to their knowledge and experience. No one can compare to our sole Creator (Elohim) and Healer (Jehovah Rapha). He is the "omni-" everything.

Another way to look at how God has *wired* his people is to look at the relationship and connection of Jesus and the church body. The apostle Paul writes to the people of Colossae about whom Christ is to us and we are to Him.

In Verses 15-17 (NLT), Paul says Christ "existed before anything was created and is supreme over all creation," and that Christ "holds all creation together."

Paul explains that,

> "Christ is also the head of the church,
> which is his body.
> He is the beginning,
> supreme over all who rises from the dead.
> So he is first in everything.
> For God in all his fullness
> was pleased to live in Christ,
> and through him God reconciled
> everything to himself.
> He made peace with everything in heaven and
> on earth
> by means of Christ's blood on the cross."
> Colossians 1:18-20 (NLT)

Jesus is at the center of it all—connecting us to His power, holding all creation together, and being the head of the church (which is called the body).

Like different parts of a car or a building, if we are connected to the power source (Christ), we can individually use our gifts and do what we were created for.

The apostle Paul tells the Romans, "Just as our bodies have many parts and each part has a special function," so it is with the church body. Christ's body.

We shouldn't try to be something we were not designed to be. An elevator is not a faucet, and hallway lighting is not a water sprinkler system. Romans 12:4 (ESV) states, "For as in one [church] body we have many members, and the members do not have the same function."

Take a moment to think about your gifts and how you feel God has wired you. Are you a leader? A teacher? Are you a caregiver and compassionate? Can you manage well?

Where do you find yourself plugged in to Jesus, the power source? Worship? Studying the Word? Serving others?

Are you producing fruit?

Let that ruminate in your thoughts for a bit.

These are all questions about you. Have you ever admired someone for *their* abilities? To sing? To play a musical instrument? To solve complex problems or public speaking?

I use the word *admire*, because I mean *to recognize and respect* their ability. I don't mean to *envy* their ability. When we do that, we cross over into *jealousy or resentment* which aren't righteous behaviors.

One example, I admit, is I wish I could sing. I wish I could hit the notes and stir an audience the way someone like Italian tenor Andrea Bocelli does. His voice resounds into the depths of my heart...but I don't envy him. I don't wish I could take his gifts away from him, so I could have them. God planned and wired Bocelli to be who he is, just as God planned and wired me to be who I am, and He wired you to be who you are.

Bocelli found his "voice" to be an outlet for his faith. In an interview with Colm Flynn for *EWTN News In Depth* (2021), Andrea Bocelli acknowledged his voice as a divine gift.

"Things happen because there is a grand design," Bocelli said. In the interview, he reflected on his early ability to sing as a boy and how "in demand" he was to sing–at parties, churches, and school. He said, "It became like [his singing] was meant to be."[34]

Obviously, Bocelli's numerous musical awards and record sales reflect a fruitful career. However, Bocelli said life in this world, no matter how long it is, is insignificant if there is no eternal life.

"Everything would lose all meaning," he explained. He was talking about the life after this life. his being connected to the vine of Christ, Bocelli and his audiences have experienced and witnessed the fruitfulness of his life.

How important is your faith? Flynn asked Bocelli.

"It is a reason for life."

Bocelli put it in simple terms: "I do not believe in the clock without the clockmaker."

He explained, "I don't believe anything can be achieved without someone who has designed and built it."[35]

What is *your* outlet of faith? What is God's grand design for *you*? He has one, you know.

When we connect to the ultimate source of the greatest power, Christ's power, we let Him feed and nourish our abilities. We will not only enjoy his blessings, but others can be blessed and encouraged as well.

For 3 ½ years, the twelve apostles traveling with Jesus witnessed his power to heal the sick, feed the numbers, and raise the dead. These twelve watched as Jesus called out demons, walked on water, and calmed the seas. They learned that the power that Jesus used to perform these miracles He would be giving to them later, in the form of the Holy Spirit. That same power He gave to them, He gives to us–who have accepted Jesus as our Lord and Savior.

Jesus speaks to the apostles in John 14:16-17 (NLT):

> "And I will ask the Father, and he will give you another Advocate, who will never leave you. He is the Holy Spirit, who leads into all truth. The world cannot receive him, because it isn't looking for him and doesn't recognize him. But you know him, because he lives with you now and later will be in you."

The apostles lived with Jesus. They saw power through his words and actions. During his ministry, Jesus showed the apostles the power within Him. He was closely connected to these particular twelve men. Nearing his crucifixion, Jesus tells them that they too will be given the power through the Holy Spirit.

After Christ is crucified, dies, and is raised from the dead, He appears to them "from time to time, and he proves to them in many ways that he was actually alive" (Acts 1:3 NLT).

When the time came for Jesus to ascend to heaven, "[He] was taken up into a cloud while they were watching, and they could no longer see him" (Acts 1:9 NLT). And, after Jesus has joined his Father in heaven and the apostles have gathered together, the power of the Holy Spirit is given to each of them.

I stress to you, His *power* was given to *each* of them:

> "[There] was a sound from heaven like the roaring of a mighty windstorm, and it filled the house where they were sitting. Then, what looked like flames or tongues of fire appeared and settled on each of them. And everyone present was filled with the Holy Spirit and began speaking in other languages, as the Holy Spirit gave them ability." Acts 2:2-4 (NLT)

No words, no science, no amount of money can lasso or clone the power of the Holy Spirit.

Standing in the streets, the diverse crowd in Jerusalem begins hearing voices speaking loudly to each person, in their own languages. The people are bewildered, amazed, and perplexed. Such power is not understood.

What would you make of a gathering of men, shouting out loudly in different languages? Wouldn't you suspect the men were drunk, too? Maybe question your hearing or your sanity?

Peter explains to the crowd exactly what has happened. God, "by doing powerful miracles, wonders, and signs through him… knew what would happen and his prearranged plan was carried out" (Acts 2:22-23 NLT).

Jesus is crucified, died, and buried, and on the third day, He rises again, according to the Word, and now He is seated at the right hand of the Father. The "noise" that the people in the streets are hearing is the Holy Spirit being poured out upon the apostles, the vine connecting to the branches, just as Jesus foretold.

Peter explains to the people in the streets what the Lord has done. They respond, *What should we do?*

He tells them to repent of their sins, turn to God, be baptized in the name of Jesus for the forgiveness of their sins, and receive the power of the Holy Spirit themselves.

He tells them to turn to the Vine.

The Holy Spirit produces in us fruit of all kinds–love, joy, peace, patience, kindness, goodness, faithfulness, gentleness, and self-control (Galatians 5:22)–fruit that He can put to use.

If you choose to follow Jesus, you are to do the same: repent of your sins, turn to God, be baptized, and receive the Holy Spirit. This is your connection to the Vine.

Do not be surprised or afraid of what the Holy Spirit may give you the ability to do.

Be you, in all of your wonderful glory. Use your gifts and be fruitful.

You are wired to be a follower of Christ. God gave you that ability. Connect yourself to Jesus. Communicate with Him. Draw from His endless power within you.

Finally, and most importantly, spread the word. Tell others what He has done for you. Help them make a connection with the Father.

The same Spirit that gives you ability also gives you confidence and courage. Maybe you'll be blessed to see it to completion. Maybe not. But, we already talked about that.

I invite you to join me in using words from "The Vine and the Branches" by Josh Hoffert as part of prayer:

Heavenly Father, I am but deadwood, disconnected wires ready for the fire, unless I connect myself to you through your Son, Jesus. When I am one with Jesus, his power is in me. In the same way a vine gives form and life to the branch, my attachment to Christ forms me and makes a difference in the type of person that I am becoming. Jesus as the Vine is actively cleansing me by his Word.

Union with Christ comes in personal moments with Him, much the way He lived and shared intimacy with the Father. When I contain the life of the vine, his words abide within me. And as his words abide in me, I can say that I abide in him.36

I call upon the power of Your Holy Spirit to give me the fruit and abilities You want me to have. May I bring others to know You by the fruit they see me produce. Amen

Application: Lights Out

It was like a scene out of *The Natural*.[37]

My daughter Mari and I sat in the living room watching and listening to the thunder and lightning, grandly performing outside. Flashes and rumbles went on for some time. As the storm intensified, I pulled the lace curtain back. At that exact moment, a white bolt of lightning struck the hickory tree, towering in our front yard. The top branches exploded and showered down in chunks and splinters around the base.

We screamed in unison.

We both felt a charge go up our feet and throughout our body.

I let go of the curtain like it was a live wire. "Oh my God, did you feel that?!"

The tree top was on fire. Branches and bark were scattered. But, the tree was still standing…mostly.

We wondered if we had actually been shocked.

After the storm, my husband and I examined the tree and cleaned up the mess. A burn mark ran from the top of the tree to the ground. Would the tree survive?

Within a year, the "divinely topped" tree came down during another storm, taking nearby power lines with it.

We've gone hours and even days without power.

My husband and I have mentioned several times that a generator might not be a bad idea.

What sources of backup lighting or power do you have in your home?

_____   _____

_____   _____

_____   _____

_____   _____

If you lost power in your car, what emergency lighting do you have or power do you have?

_____   _____

_____   _____

_____   _____

_____   _____

Why do we do this?

Darkness can make many people anxious. The same room in the daytime feels so different in the dark night. Obstacles become more of a threat in darkness, and seem like a possible enemy. We reach out to find something recognizable and walk more slowly to avoid hurting ourselves.

One candle, one flashlight, or one match breaks the darkness. We are drawn to light because it helps us see more clearly.

From Genesis to Revelation, Scripture talks about light.

Read Genesis Chapter 1.

- Which existed first–light or darkness?

_____

- On what day of creation did God separate light and darkness?

  _____

- Who did God create light for? Us or Him?

  _____

Day Four of creation focuses a great deal on "light." Circle each time the word *light* is written:

> "And God said, 'Let there be lights in the expanse of the heavens to separate the day from the night. And let them be for signs and for seasons, and for days and years, and let them be lights in the expanse of the heavens to give light upon the earth.' And it was so. And God made the two great lights—the greater light to rule the day and the lesser light to rule the night— and the stars. And God set them in the expanse of the heavens to give light on the earth, to rule over the day and over the night, and to separate the light from the darkness. And God saw that it was good. And there was evening and there was morning, the fourth day." Genesis 1:14-19 (ESV)

We learn in elementary school that the moon does not emit light on its own. It reflects the light from the sun–in slivers, quarters, and full moons. Nonetheless, that reflected light is to guide us through darkness.

The word *light* is used over 200 times in scripture, regardless of the version we read (Christian Bible Reference Site). We learn:

- the Word of God is a light to our path (Psalm 119)
- our Lord lightens our darkness (Psalm 18:28)
- the Lord is my light and salvation that I don't need to be afraid (Psalm 27:1)

1 John 1:5 (ESV) says, "God is light, and in him is no darkness at all."

We see darkness differently than God does. He brought light into the world for us, for the places we will dwell. Each day, creation is affected by light. Earth and the seas are affected by the sun and moon. Vegetation and creatures of the land and sea and sky all respond to light and darkness. We humans, male and female, depend on light.

To explain who He is to the Pharisees, Jesus told them, "I am the light of the world. Whoever follows me will not walk in darkness, but will have the light of life" (John 8:12 ESV).

Even when Jesus was crucified, the Light of the world was not extinguished. On the third day, He rose again, later ascended to heaven, and now his light shines from the throne.

Jesus' beloved apostle John describes for us in the book of Revelation the New Jerusalem our God has prepared for us.

Read Revelation 21.

Heaven and Earth are going to be different.

What will no longer exist?

_____ _____
_____ _____
_____ _____
_____ _____

Consider how God's design of heaven differs from what we saw in Genesis Chapter 1. Revelation tells us the walls will be of jasper, pure gold, and clear glass. The foundations in heaven will be adorned in jewels, and the gates of perfect pearl.

And, why will there be no street lights?

Verse 23, "[The] city has no need of sun or moon to shine on it, for the glory of God gives it light, and its lamp is the Lamb." God, in all His glory, *is* light!

We have a choice to turn from darkness and turn to the light, from the power of Satan to the power of God (Acts 26:18 ESV). Several times, the apostle Paul writes that we were living in darkness, but the moment we accepted Christ as our Lord and Savior, we decided to follow the light and *be* the light.

> "For at one time you were darkness, but now you are light in the Lord. Walk as children of light."
> Ephesians 5:8-9 (ESV)

I have a challenge for everyone this week. First, memorize the above verse from Ephesians 5:8-9. Then, each time this week that you turn on the lights—in your home, work, car—recite this verse to yourself. Think of the power God has given you. Let His light shine through you for you are a child of light!

Mark at the Colosseum, Rome, Italy–2006

Chapter Eight

The Façade

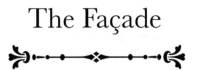

> "Do not let your adorning be external...but let your
> adorning be the hidden person of the heart with the
> imperishable beauty of a gentle and quiet spirit, which
> in God's sight is very precious."
> I Peter 3:3-4 (ESV)

*I*f you're close to my age, you likely watched plenty of commercials when you were young. During those days before Netflix and pay channels, I memorized what was on a Big Mac, how to spell b-o-l-o-g-n-a, and when it was time to make the donuts. I also learned from commercials the prerequisite to talking to an attractive stranger–make sure you don't have dandruff because "you never get a second chance to make a first impression."[38]

I learned early on when you have an opportunity to attract attention, it's better to make it positive rather than negative. So, for goodness sake, buy the shampoo.

The word *facade* is French, meaning "face." And, the facade of a building is the first thing people see. It's the book cover. The first impression.

"A great façade has the power to grab attention and keep it. Unique facades offer their occupants the opportunity to express their personality and unique style and to stand out from the surrounding buildings, thus creating a point of differentiation."[39]

I am much better at faces than names. Something about the smile and eyes leave a more lasting impression on me. They are the first things I record to memory and can recall, long after the person's name.

Architects and builders want to do the same. They strive for their work to leave a lasting, positive impression. Yes, the name of a business is vital, but the impression of it can last. Under the surface, buildings are brick and mortar, steel and concrete, windows and wood. Yet, the covering, colors, and design of the building front, or facade, are the *extra-* that makes the ordinary become *extraordinary.*

Many homes and buildings stand out as truly unique. The Biltmore House, the Guggenheim Museum, the Sydney Opera House. The world is full of unique buildings.

I'd like you to picture in your mind one structure in particular–the Egyptian pyramids. Those are truly unique. Go ahead. Take your eyes off the book for a minute, and imagine the ancient pyramids of the pharaohs.

What do you *see*?

Four triangular walls? Stones tightly stacked upon one another? Slanted walls meeting at a point? A structure extending high above desert, sandy ground?

Let's try another. Try picturing the not-as-old, but ancient nonetheless, Roman Colosseum. I'll wait.

What do you see?

Are you imagining a roofless, round structure like a stadium? Rows and rows of arches and columns? Do you see missing outer portions of walls?

If not then, I bet my asking brought some of those details to your mind now.

Though the pyramids and the colosseum are roughly 2,500 years apart in age, the rulers who had them built wanted truly, one-of-a-kind, architectural wonders, for their grandeur to be seen by all and from afar. The amount of resources poured into both are unimaginable. One was to be a final resting place for a ruler, and the other to seat spectators for bloody entertainment and shows.

Did it cross your mind to picture the tunnels inside of both? Or, the concealed chambers and rooms? Did you envision ancient writings chiseled into the interior pyramid walls? Or, the gates, trap doors, or seating of the colosseum?

More than likely not. Me neither.

That's because our thoughts were more likely on the outside than the inside.

The inside of a building embodies its purpose, but the outside provides its allure, its curb appeal. Builders generally strive to make a good impression and often spend a great deal of money and time on image.

And, so do we.

Whether it's our car, home, appearance, or our social circle, we reflect a personality and unique style, even if we aren't trying to. And–if we are followers of Christ–our outward "appearance" can positively or negatively affect others' impressions of Christians and the body of the church.

I have both met and been one of *those* Christians.

When I first became a believer in Christ, I was so excited to become the person God wanted me to be. But, I realized I needed to get rid of so much unhealthy, heavy baggage. The transformation was like gutting a house. To really make a strong, lasting change, boundaries needed to be redrawn, some relationships needed to go, and I needed to rewire my thinking.

I was a real mess, but it was going to get messier before it got better.

"Do not be conformed to this world, but be transformed by the renewal of your mind, that by testing you may discern what is the will of God, what is good and acceptable and perfect" (Romans 12:2 ESV).

I went from conforming to transforming.

I shifted my attention from an outward focus to an inside one. I especially needed to get my heart right. To forgive more, give more, and not be so critical. And, it's taken years. I began rewiring my heart by reading scripture. Replacing toxic relationships with healthier ones. And, recognizing what media, places, and behaviors negatively impact me.

Charles Stanley–pastor, writer, speaker–says building or growing in our faith is like peeling back layers of an onion. Once the knowledge and experience of what Jesus has done *for* us begins growing, we will start to see what Jesus is doing *in* us. What we see still down in our heart that is unpleasing to God will make us want to "go to God and look for forgiveness and freedom," from the parts of our old self that remain. Again, like peeling an onion one layer at a time.

"Each layer represents a new area of our lives that God is working on next. We work with God to peel that layer off of our lives," Stanley says.[40]

Oftentimes, Jesus called out the Jewish leaders for this very thing. Their outward appearance, or *facade,* didn't match what was inside of them. "So you, too, outwardly appear righteous to men, but inwardly you are full of hypocrisy and lawlessness" (Matthew 23:28 NASB).

The word *facade* has a second meaning. The *Cambridge Dictionary* definition helps us understand what Jesus meant in Matthew 23 above. The Jewish leader put forth *a false **appearance** that made them* [and their practices] *seem more pious or better than they really were.*[41] False fronts, masks, guises, window dressings. The religious leaders were hypocrites.

Rather, Jesus taught that our true face should be expressed:

- **in prayer** (Matthew 6:5-8 NIV) "When you pray, do not be like the hypocrites, for they love to pray standing in the synagogues and on the street corners to be seen by men ... but when you pray, go into your room, close the door and pray to your father who is unseen."
- **in giving** (Matthew 6:2 ESV) "Thus, when you give to the needy, sound no trumpet before you, as the hypocrites do in the synagogues and in the streets, that they may be praised by others. Truly, I say to you, they have received their reward."
- **in fasting** (Matthew 6:16-18 ESV) "When you fast, don't make yourselves look sad like the hypocrites. They put a look of suffering on their faces so that people will see they are fasting. The truth is, that's all the reward they

will get. So when you fast, wash your face and make yourself look nice. Then no one will know you are fasting, except your Father, who is with you even in private. He can see what is done in private, and he will reward you."

God doesn't want what's on the outside of us to be different from what is on the inside. Jesus flat out calls it *hypocrisy*, an inciting word. He wants the heart of a believer to shine through to the outside. In our thoughts, words, and deeds.

I Samuel 16:7 (ESV) reads, "For the LORD sees not as man sees; man looks on the outward appearance, but the LORD looks on the heart."

Think again about those Egyptian pyramids and the Roman Colosseum. What were they for? One was to house the dead. The other, an open arena to watch animals and men battle to the death. Amazing buildings on the outside but death dwelled on the inside. Jesus felt similarly about the Pharisees and Jewish leaders. They were quite spectacular on the outside but dead inside. He confronted what He saw in their hearts:

"Woe to you, scribes and Pharisees, hypocrites! For you clean the outside of the cup and of the dish, but inside they are full of robbery and self-indulgence. You blind Pharisee, first clean the inside of the cup and of the dish, so that the outside of it may become clean also. Woe to you, scribes and Pharisees, hypocrites! For you are like whitewashed tombs which on the outside appear beautiful, but inside they are full of dead men's bones and all uncleanness." (Matthew 23:25-28 NIV)

We should be the same person publicly that we are privately. A reflection on the outside of what's inside. If we are light on the inside, it should show on the outside. And, if we are dead on the inside, well, we have no light that can shine.

We *are* going to fail from time to time. Charles Stanley states, "We still act out and sin against our neighbor and against God. [But when we] begin to go to God and look for forgiveness and freedom" from the old us that remains, we are peeling away just another layer that needs to be removed.[42]

Building a strong faith takes commitment in heart, mind, and soul.

When God looks at you, He sees the unique design He himself created. You have the brick and mortar, framing and wiring, all the power you need to house the most precious guest–the Holy Spirit–right within you. Let the Spirit search your heart and look for anything in you that's not pleasing to God. Ask God to remove the unnecessary, useless connections you've made to the world and its idols and to peel away the worldly facade and replace it with beauty that shines through.

Before we pray, I want to share something written by James, the half-brother of Jesus. James' faith grew *after* he saw Jesus risen from the grave. James was a doubter. "For even his brothers did not believe in him" (John 7:5). However, James' heart changed when he saw a risen Jesus. In his letter, James announced himself as "a servant of God and the Lord Jesus Christ" (James 1:1 NIV).

James had much to say about how the faith we have will produce good works. However, those works do *not* produce faith. One particular message from James is in Chapter 2:1-4 (NIV):

"My brothers and sisters, believers in our glorious Lord Jesus Christ must not show favoritism. Suppose a man comes into your meeting wearing a gold ring and fine clothes, and a poor man in filthy old clothes also comes in. If you show special attention to the man wearing fine clothes and say, 'Here's a good seat for you,' but say to the poor man, 'You stand there' or "Sit on the floor by my feet,' have you not discriminated among yourselves and become judges with evil thoughts?"

Might we ask ourselves how often we judge someone by their facade? The clothes they wear, the color of their skin, and place they come from?

I invite you to say this prayer with me:

*L*ord God, I know I can be judgmental. I see someone or something, and I form thoughts based on what I see on the outside. Thoughts that can be so different from what YOU see on the inside. You didn't shy away from lepers or others seen as "unclean." You not only talked with them. You also touched them and healed them from the inside out. You dined with sinners, forgave adulterers, welcomed the children, and turned the hearts of the many toward You. You love the Gentile as well as the Jew.

I don't want to be like a Pharisee. I don't want to LOOK the part of a believer but not LiVE IT on the inside. Start with my heart, Lord. Peel away those areas of my old self that need to be removed. May my facade reflect the light of Christ inside and draw others toward it, toward You, and not me. Amen

Application: Spiritual Imaging

Do you remember scraped knees, bruises, and bumps as a kid? Did you ever have stitches or a broken bone? I had my fair share. When I was little, I played hard.

Sometimes, we have X-rays, CT scans, and MRIs to see what is happening below the surface. ER doctors, specialists, or family physicians may have a hunch, but to truly know, medical imaging can detect internal damage and the extent.

However, there's not a machine that can spot what our human spirit may be suffering. Dr. David Roger Clawson writes for *Psychology Today* that we not only experience physical threats to our safety but also spiritual ones. Attacks on our emotions, social well-being, and finances, for example, "have similar effects to physical threat and injury."[43]

Do any of the following ever affect your spirit, or heart? Circle any that do:

Politics	Racism	War	Drug use
Income	Social media	Health care	Nationalism
Gangs	Career	Illness	Relationships
Child care	Loss	Aging	

Any one of these can cause spiritual illness, something that threatens your security.

Lisa Iannucci writes that "a building facade is more than just the face it shows to the street–it's a protective barrier against the elements and an integral part of the building's structure."[44] We need protection and security inside and out.

Remember what the apostle Paul tells us in Ephesians 6:12 (NLT):

> "For we are not fighting against flesh-and-blood enemies, but against evil rulers and authorities of the unseen world, against mighty powers in this dark world, and against evil spirits in the heavenly places."

Paul tells us that each day, we are to prepare ourselves for the outward attack from the evil spirits and darkness that want to affect us inside, to affect our place of safety. "Therefore put on the full armor of God, so that when the day of evil comes, you may be able to stand your ground, and after you have done everything, to stand" (Ephesians 6:13 NIV).

Read Ephesians 6:14-17. The full, protective armor of God includes:

1. The belt of _____
2. The breastplate of _____
3. The sandals of _____
4. The shield of _____
5. The helmet of _____
6. The sword of _____

Clawson says, "As we are an inherently spiritual species, we frequently fear a spiritual death as much as a physical death."[45]

So, what do we do about it?

Dr. Clawson says to move people away from the threat and towards safety. He states that, "Health does not always come from medicine. Most of the time it comes from peace of mind, peace of heart, and peace of soul."[46]

The key word above is *peace.*

On Jesus' last night with his apostles, He tells them that it is time for Him to leave them and join his Father in heaven. He promises the Advocate–the Holy Spirit–will come to them. "I am leaving you with a gift–peace of mind and heart. And the peace I give is the gift the world cannot give. So don't be troubled or afraid" (John 14:27 NLT).

We may struggle in spirit because of the world we live in. But, God will not only dress us in the full armor of God, should we choose to accept it, but also fill us with the Holy Spirit, that will indwell us and encourage us to not to be afraid.

If you have not accepted Jesus as your Lord and Savior, the Holy Spirit has yet to light upon you. You are fighting the battles of the world solo. As Iannucci states, "In the case of buildings, problems never get better on their own."[47] Jesus lived, died, and rose so you and I don't have to fight alone. Jesus will never leave us nor forsake us. What He said to the apostles on his last night, He is speaking to all of us–

"I am leaving you with a gift–peace of mind and heart."
John 14:27 (NLT)

If you haven't accepted that gift of Spirit till now, it is not too late.

Chapter Nine

Simple Furnishings

"No one lights a lamp and then covers it with a bowl or
hides it under a bed. A lamp is placed on a stand, where
it can be seen by all who enter the house."
Luke 8:16 (NLT)

*O*nce, we traveled to Rome on a business trip for my husband. After two exhausting days of flights and layovers, we were stunned when we walked into the hotel room. A tiny table set in the corner. No chair. No lamp. No television. The room wasn't much bigger than the hallway in our house. We literally could stand in the middle of the room and touch opposite walls with our hands. Not only that, the bed was much smaller than the traditional twin bed in our spare bedroom. The hotel couldn't make any changes that night, so my husband and I squeezed together lying on our sides. Neither of us would turn over for fear the other might fall off.

It was a memorable experience. Funny now. Not so much then.

Looking back, other amenities like a kitchenette, jacuzzi tub, and sitting area would have been amazing; they certainly would have made the stay more comfortable. And, if the property had a pool and restaurant, that would have been all the better. But honestly, after our long travel experience, the bed was all we really needed. I had never considered a bed, even a small one, such a luxury until then.

Telling that story reminds me of another young couple that had traveled for days. When they finally arrived where they were going, both were exhausted. They, too, needed a place to stay. However, the town was crowded. Every room was booked. There were no vacancies. Nothing. They were desperate for a place to rest. They would take anything.

Anything.

Joseph and Mary were required to report to Bethlehem from Nazarene. It took nearly a week by foot and donkey. When they reached their destination, no rooms were available, and Mary was especially exhausted. She was nine-months pregnant.

Shortly after they arrived in the city, Mary went into labor. These new parents delivered their baby in a stable, a place intended to keep animals. The story of Jesus' birth explains that a manger–or feeding trough–became the Son of God's first bed.

I think of where Mary laid and birthed her son, and I am humbled. A stable floor. Ground trod by animals. She would have been overwhelmed by the luxury of our small room and bed in Rome.

Another bed crude to most of us, though typical in biblical days, is described in Genesis 28. Jacob, on a trip from Beersheba to Harran, stops along his journey and must sleep under the stars. Scripture says in Verse 11 (NIV) that when "he reached a certain place, he stopped for the night because the sun had set." Again, no place for a person to stay.

"Taking one of the stones there, he put it under his head and he lay down to sleep."

A stone for a pillow. Jacob sleeps on the ground, a rock beneath his head.

In the story, Jacob has a dream. God tells Jacob that He will give Jacob and his descendants the land where he is lying. Jacob awakens and shouts, "How awesome is this place! This is none other than the house of God; this is the gate of heaven!" (Genesis 28:13-17 NIV).

Jacob's bed that night becomes a blessed place for not only Jacob but all of his people to follow.

Jacob takes his very "pillow," sets it up as a pillar, and anoints it with oil. He vows that if God keeps him safe and provides for his needs, "this stone that I have set up as a pillar will be God's house, and all that you give me I will give you a tenth" (Genesis 28:22 NIV).

Jacob anoints his resting place and commits it to be "God's house."

Hang onto that idea. We will return to it later.

Furniture of the home is not described in much detail in scripture. According to the *International Standard Bible Encyclopedia*, "By way of information regarding the general furniture of the house little is said directly in scripture. The chamber built for Elisha upon the wall contained a bed, a table, a seat, and lampstand. This was doubtless the furnishing of most bedrooms when it could be afforded."[48]

A bed, a table, a seat, and a lampstand.

A bed is listed as one of the most important pieces of furniture in the home. Most of us spend 25-30% of each day in bed. When a person is beginning with an empty home, *The Washington Post* quotes designer Bryon Risdon, "Focus on the rooms you use the most. The bedroom is very important. It should be sort of a safe haven or a respite."[42] One thing we most certainly want our "space" to be is a comfortable place to rest. A bed or couch can help meet that need.

For many around the world, a sheet of cardboard, a park bench, a sidewalk, an abandoned building floor, a carseat, or a storage unit may be where homeless men, women, and children lay their heads at night.

Consider this: For 3 ½ years, Jesus was *homeless*.

Throughout his ministry, Jesus depended on the Father for provision. Jesus carried with Him no possessions. He slept outdoors, and He slept as a guest in others' homes.

Jesus stated, "Foxes have dens to live in, and birds have nests, but the Son of Man has no place even to lay his head" (Luke 9:58, Matthew 8:20 NLT).

Whether at someone's home, in a boat, in a garden, on a hill, or in a manger, Jesus made his bed.

Throughout scripture, a bed is more than just part of the backdrop. It's interwoven into the story. It's where we find people in moments of death, resurrection, seduction, healing, visions, worship, and blessings.

- (In Genesis 49) Isaac, on his **deathbed**, was tricked into giving his **blessing** to Jacob rather than Esau, causing conflict and division.
- (In Acts 5:15, Mark 6:55, Matthew 9:6, John 5:8-12) Brought upon **cots, mats, and pallets**, the sick reach out to Jesus or Peter for **healing**.

- (In Hebrews 13:4) The writer tells believers that marriage should be honored by all and the **marriage bed** kept **pure.**
- (In Mark 4:38) While Jesus was asleep in the **stern of the boat** lying upon a cushion, his disciples were **tested** by the rising storm.
- (In I Kings 17-24) Elijah laid a widow's lifeless son upon a **bed,** stretched himself upon the boy, and cried out to the Lord until He **restored life** to the boy.
- (In John 11:1-44) Jesus called to Lazarus who had lain dead for four days in **a tomb** to come out. **Arise.** Lazarus appeared, hands and feet were bound by linen, and face wrapped with a cloth.
- (In Daniel 7:1-3) Lying in **his bed,** Daniel had a **dream with visions** of four beasts, representing kingdoms–rising and falling–with the last being the Most High reign of the Lord, who will judge all of mankind.

We all lay our head down to sleep somewhere. In a car, plane, hotel, or home. Maybe outdoors. It could be morning, afternoon, or night. No matter how big or small our space–something will become a bed for us.

Light is another vital element for a home. As a furnishing, it sets the very tone and feel for the room.

There's a scene in the 1984 movie *The Natural*[50] where a mysterious, rookie baseball player Roy Hobbs walks into the dark office of his team owner known as the Judge. When Hobbs (played by Robert Redford) enters the Judge's office, Hobbs hesitates. Only one, small, table lamp is lit in the corner. Hobbs enters and tries to adapt to the darkness.

His boss, the Judge, explains that as a child, he was afraid of the dark, but he later disciplined himself to the dark, and now the Judge says that he "prefers" darkness.

Hobbs' response is, "The only thing I know about the dark is you can't see in it."

We aren't nocturnal creatures. Yes, our eyes adapt somewhat to the darkness but not like an owl or a possum or raccoon who sees keenly in the absence of light. We don't thrive in darkness.

Darkness can represent more than just the absence of physical, earthly light. Dozens of verses in the Bible use *darkness* to symbolize a person being lost spiritually, or without the Light of Jesus in his life.

When Hobbs is about to walk out of the Judge's office, he defiantly flips the switch, turning the lights on. The Judge yells, "You come back here and turn off that infernal light!"

Infernal light.

A bit of an oxymoron. *Infernal* means something "hellish" or "damned," and *light* is something "illuminating" or "a beacon." Putting the two words together produces not only a powerful expletive for the Judge, but also shows how he not only prefers darkness over light, but he is *cursing* the light. This character cheats, coerces, and threatens his adversaries. He is anything but virtuous. Hobbs is just the opposite. He has brought light to the struggling team, refuses the Judge's bribe, and sacrifices his health for the good of the others. Hobbs' flip of the lightswitch shows which he's chosen–light over darkness. This incites the Judge who is exposed for who he is.

We have that choice too. To live in spiritual light or darkness?

One of the many names for Jesus is "Light of the World." In John 8:12 (ESV), Jesus says, "I am the light of the world.

Whoever follows me will not walk in darkness, but will have the light of life."

Each room in our home needs light *if* we don't want to stumble. If. We don't have to use the lights. Many times, I have thought I could manage on my own walking through my house. Sometimes I can. Other times, an obstacle can be in my path, and I can regret my choice. Whether on the ceiling, tables, stands, or wall, light is able to spread throughout a room but only if we choose to use it.

Unlike the Judge in the movie, most of us are drawn to light. We feel safer, and our fears fade in light.

In Psalm 119:105 (ESV), the psalmist writes, "Your word is a lamp for my feet, a light on my path." Without a light, we can stumble accidentally or even intentionally. The Word of God is a beacon. It can enlighten us to what we should see as stumbling blocks in our life. Without knowing God, without interacting with Him through his Word, we are grasping in the dark for what feels good and feels right. It can put us in harm's way.

Being a Follower of Jesus, *WE* become light in a dark world because we have the very Spirit of God inside of us, and we are not to hide that light. We are to *project, attract,* and *offer it* to others. Jesus says that the Light, or Spirit within us, is like a "town built on a hill [that] cannot be hidden" (Matthew 5:14 NIV). Homes contain light, businesses use light, and streets project light. All can be seen from afar.

I ask you, how bright is your *light*? To you, who have accepted Christ as your Lord and Savior, do you feel people can tell? Are you carrying the light of Christ in you?

There should be no doubt.

There are times my light feels pretty low. But, even a dim light can break the darkness. I often examine what I'm doing to stay plugged into the source. Am I worshiping? Reading my Bible? How's my prayer life? The Light of Christ never runs low. My disengagement from Him becomes something not only I realize but others who know me see, too.

Luke 8:16 (NLT) records Jesus explaining, "No one lights a lamp and then covers it with a bowl or hides it under a bed. A lamp is placed on a stand, where it can be seen by all who enter the house."

Shine your light brightly, not only for your own benefit, but for others. Don't try to conceal it. Don't be afraid of your faith being seen or on display. Jesus wasn't afraid to spread the Word to his followers, and He didn't hide from anyone–especially those who wanted to persecute Him. We, too, are to fear not.

Consider this: there will be no need for lamps or lights in the New Jerusalem that awaits. "The city has no need of sun or moon, for the glory of God illuminates the city and the Lamb is its light" (Revelation 21:23 NLT).

The apostle John says in Revelation that all nations in heaven "will walk in light" and there will be no night.

> "And there will be no night there–no need for lamps or sun–for the **Lord God** will shine on them."
> (my emphasis, Revelation 22:5 NLT)

The glory of the Lord will be all the light that eternity will ever have or need, and we will be able to look into the very face of God.

We have numerous pieces of furniture and possessions filling our homes. We drive past storage units that contain the overflow. Some people buy bigger homes to house their belongings, and others let it collect to a level of hoarding.

I ask, *What do we really need? What should our home be for?* I'm not asking what the world tells us that it should be, but what the Father would tell us it should be?

I believe if we are blessed with a place to call home, it's a place of refuge, provision, and light. A beacon calling out to others that God provides in this place.

Over the years, my family has welcomed many, many people into our home. Maybe you have too. Food is usually part of the plan. We sit around a table, eat, and talk.

Your home, like mine, is likely full of different tables. I hadn't realized how many I have until I began writing this paragraph. Kitchen tables, dining room tables, coffee tables, end tables. Bedside tables. Couch tables. There are tables and stands in our house that I can't even give a specific name. They are simply the "round table" and the "tall table." They are similar yet different. However, the table that seems to draw the most attention is in our dining room.

Our house isn't huge, but we've squeezed some sizable groups in our space. We've noticed, however, when friends or family are over, for some reason we almost always find ourselves gathered in the kitchen and around the dining room table.

Sometimes, our guests never make it to the living room or family room. We sit around the dining room table–eating, talking, celebrating, playing games, and studying. We cried and prayed together around that table. Mulled over life decisions and heartbreaks around that table.

The table seats six, but it's not unheard of to have 10 of us around it, squeezing folks in at the corners. It's also not strange to see a toddler or two in a grown-up's lap. My husband and I laugh after everyone leaves, and we realize the folding tables we set up in the living room were never used.

Why?

Why does this happen?

I think it's because we want to be one body, gathered together.

We probably don't give the tables in our homes much thought, but like beds, their presence in the Bible shouldn't be looked at as just part of the setting. They literally are part of the story and illustration.

Tables throughout scripture serve different purposes, too. Some of the first tables of mention were used in the Tabernacle.

In Exodus 25:8-9 (NLT), God tells Moses, "Have the people of Israel build me a holy sanctuary so I can live among them. You must build this Tabernacle and its furnishings exactly according to the pattern I will show you."

God instructs Moses what and how to build the place of worship and then what furnishings He wants for what purpose. For example, "There were two rooms in the Tabernacle. In the first room were a lampstand, a table, and sacred loaves of bread on the table. This room was called the Holy Place" (Hebrews 9:2 NLT).

Exodus 25:23-40 outlines God's pattern for the lampstand and the table for the Holy Place. Other containers–bowls, pans, pitchers, and jars–would also be kept on the table to be used in pouring out liquid offerings.

The purpose of the table was to honor God's provision. God commanded, "[Then place] the Bread of Presence on the table to remain before me at all times."

This table, in design and purpose, was to honor God–by keeping "His ongoing provision in front of his people and remind them of His enduring holy attention to them."[51]

Another table showing God's provision is first mentioned in Luke 22:8.

It was Passover time. Jesus knew priests and religious leaders were planning his death. Judas Iscariot was about to betray Him. The "Passover Lamb" was about to be sacrificed.

Jesus sent Peter and John ahead and said, "Go and prepare the Passover meal, so we can eat it together" (NLT).

"When the time came, Jesus and the apostles sat down together at the table. Jesus said, 'I have been very eager to eat this Passover meal with you before my suffering begins. For I tell you now that I won't eat this meal again until its meaning is fulfilled in the Kingdom of God.'" Luke 22:14-16 (NLT)

The bread and wine served by Jesus at this table became the sacraments from that night on, for his apostles and all believers who accept Him as their Lord and Savior. They remind and represent this one night, Jesus' offering himself up for us as a sacrifice for our sins, and his dying on the cross. Churches and homes now prepare a table, to observe the body and blood of Christ, sacrificed for our atonement.

I invite you…gather at the table. Jesus calls you to Him and has prepared a place for you. And, one day, we will all gather at a great banquet in his presence.

I try to envision the greatness of this gathering and all those who have passed before us, believers of all nations and times. Together, we will live in God's presence, his peace, and his glory.

A bed, a lamp, and a table. Three simple furnishings that offer rest, direction, and provision. What more do we need?

I invite you to join me in this prayer:

*Heavenly Father, You tell us to lay up for ourselves treasures **in heaven**, for everything on earth will one day be gone–to rust, moth, or thieves.*

Open our eyes to the stewardship we have been given, for everything belongs to you. We are just borrowing it. Jesus, you say, those who can be trusted with a little, can be trusted with much. Don't let us misinterpret what that means. He who dies with the most stuff does NOT win!

May three, particular pieces of furniture–a bed, a lamp, and a table–remind us of the Words and works of You, the prophets, Your Son Jesus, and the disciples. May we lie down at night, with peace and not malice in our hearts. May the Light of the Holy Spirit always shine through us and direct us, and may Your table offering remind us of Your presence and provision and sacrifice. Amen

Application: A Place at the Table

The *Cenacolo Vinciano* is found in Milan, Italy. You more likely know it as *The Last Supper*, painted by Leonardo da Vinci. The mural was painted on the northern wall of the refectory, or the dining hall, of the Dominican Convent of the Santa Maria delle Grazie. DaVinci, using oil on plaster, positioned Jesus and his twelve disciples at a long table. Jesus is in the center of the image and six of his disciples are on his left and six on his right. All are on one side of a single table, facing forward and talking in small groups.[52]

The Renaissance artist didn't paint chairs in the mural, however, the height of the table might suggest the thirteen men were seated.

This is just one detail Da Vinci got wrong.

In an article for *In Touch Ministries*, Kayla Yiu reports, "Jesus and the disciples weren't sitting that night. They were reclining."[53]

Reclining was customary of Jesus' day. The Greeks practiced eating at low tables. They propped themselves up on pillows, lay on their left side, and ate with their right hand. The Romans later adopted this posture.[54]

Throughout scripture, reclining or lying was done at a table.

- (Matthew 9:10) While Jesus was reclining at dinner, sinners and tax collectors joined Him at Matthew's home.
- (John 12:2) While Jesus was reclining at the table with Lazarus, Mary began pouring expensive perfume on Jesus' feet.

- (Luke 7:36) Jesus was invited by a Pharisee to dine with him, and Jesus reclined at the Pharisee's table.
- (Mark 16:14) After Jesus's death, burial and resurrection, He appeared to his eleven disciples, who were reclining at the table, and He scorned them for doubting witnesses who had seen Him.

Earlier, Jesus asked the question of his disciples at the Passover Seder Meal,

> "For who is greater, the one who reclines at the table or the one who serves?" Luke 22:27 (NASB)

Who do you think is greater? The server or the one being served? Think of places where someone comes to *serve* you. List examples:

_____   _____

_____   _____

_____   _____

Circle any of those above where **you** have served someone in that same capacity. (For example, a waitress has served you, and you have served as a waitress.)

Jesus answers his question with another question,

> "For who is greater, the one who reclines at the table or the one who serves? **Is it not the one who reclines at the table?**"

Is the restaurant guest greater or the waiter?

The world does not regard greatness the way Jesus does. The world sees greatness by the home we live in, the car we drive, the job we have, and possessions we accumulate. Greatness, too, may be judged by the number of workers who serve you.

If we want to be greater or "first" in the eyes of God, we need to make ourselves less, or "last." Jesus did not come into the world as a powerful political leader who ruled from a throne. No, He was born in a stable, rode into Jerusalem on a donkey, washed his disciples' feet, and allowed himself to be spat upon and beaten. The Son of God was crucified at the hands of Roman soldiers. With all of the authority given to Him by his Father in heaven, Jesus followed the will of God. He put our salvation ahead of his own life.

Jesus saw greatness not in kings and rulers but in humble servants.

> "[The] greatest among you should be like the youngest, and the one who rules like the one who serves. For who is greater, the one who is at the table or the one who serves? Is it not the one who is at the table? But I am among you as one who serves." Luke 22: 26-27 (NIV)

Jesus serves. We are to do likewise.

Are you the one reclining or the one serving? The one humbling yourself or showing others your "greatness"?

Another place where chairs were not used, or even present, was in the Tabernacle of Moses. Theology writer Alex Philip explains, "The Bible indicates that, for priests serving in the tabernacle, there was no sitting on the job either."[55]

Hebrews 10:11 reads, "Day after day, every priest **stands** and performs his religious duties; again and again, he offers the same sacrifices, which can never take away sins" (my emphasis, NIV).

The Tabernacle furnishings included:

> "...an altar, a large basin for washing, curtains, a table, an ark, and a lamp stand. Interestingly, there is **no chair** in the tabernacle. Dan Phillips observes that the reason for the absence of a chair in the tabernacle is... the work [of priests] never ended." [56](my emphasis)

The work of priests never ended...*until* the death, burial, and resurrection of Jesus Christ. Sacrifice for the atonement of sins never has to be repeated because the Lamb of Christ was the last and only sacrifice forever.

If.

If we accept what He offers us.

> "But when **this priest** [Jesus] had offered for all time one sacrifice for sins, he sat down at the right hand of God, and since that time he waits for his enemies to be made his footstool. For by one sacrifice he has made perfect **forever** those who are being made holy." Hebrews 10:12-14 (my emphasis, NIV)

Jesus *sits* and waits. His enemies become His footstool.

Are you "being made holy"? "Made perfect forever"?

You can't make yourself holy. *You* can't make yourself perfect. That can only be done through Christ our redeemer.

Listen to "God is on the Throne"[57] by We the Kingdom.

The next time Jesus will appear–when it's time–He will leave the throne where He has been sitting and waiting, and He will come for all God's children.

Chapter Ten

The Spirit Inside

" I will give you a new heart and put a new spirit in you; I will remove from you your heart of stone and give you a heart of flesh. And I will put my Spirit in you..."
Ezekiel 36:26-27 (NIV)

*I*f you ask people who live a little southeast of my hometown, they can probably tell you about one particular house built near the main highway. This two-story home with a southern-view of hills and farm fields began construction in 1999. As local travelers and neighbors drove past, they could visualize it coming together.

Dirt had been excavated; a foundation poured. Framing was up, and trusses set. Exterior walls, windows, roofing installed. Brick and shingles finished the outside. It seemed as though it wouldn't be long before the interior would likely be ready.

And then, everything stopped.

The dirt driveway, leading to the house, was never smoothed or covered. An excavator stayed parked beside the house, and the front door never had a porch built. The second-story exit had nowhere to go. Lights never came on. There was no movement in or outside of the house. The weeds and grass took over the 20-plus acres around the property.

The home sat empty for years.

And years.

And years.

It's been more than two decades, and the house has never been occupied. In fact, the house recently changed hands, and the seller gave it a new look with a roof change and a paint job.

Still, no one has ever moved in.

Many ask, *What's the story with that house?*

Why *would* someone build a home and let it sit empty?

Many tales and rumors have become legends about that vacant house by the highway, but no matter how beautiful, spacious, or expensive the place is, it hasn't been used for what it was built for… at least not yet.

Hebrews 3:3-7 (NIV) reads,

" … the builder of a house has greater honor than the house itself. For every house is built by someone, but God is the builder of everything. 'Moses was faithful as a servant in all God's house,' bearing witness to what would be spoken by God in the future. But Christ is faithful as the Son over God's house. And we are his house, if indeed we hold firmly to our confidence and the hope in which we glory."

The writer of Hebrews says God builds all things. Obviously, we are included in that. But, it's not the house that deserves the praise. It's the builder.

But, the question is: *Why?* Why are we built at all?

The answer: To have a relationship with the Father and to glorify Him.

In the beginning, we had a relationship with the Father... until the fall of Adam. It's through Jesus Christ and the Holy Spirit that we can again.

Writer and teacher April Motl states that "one day we will wake up to the soul-fulfillment of seeing God's face and reflecting on him just as we were always designed to do."[58]

Our design was and is to reflect on and look toward the Father. To speak with Him. To walk in His presence. To spend our life now and in eternity later glorifying Him.

Hebrews 3 says Moses was faithful as a servant in God's house, Jesus is faithful as a Son in God's house, and as God's house we are faithful to Him, "the builder of everything," if we hold firmly to our confidence and hope in Christ.

We aren't born with a Jesus-Holy Spirit relationship, and we aren't forced to let Him into our "house." Accepting who Jesus is and what He did for us on the cross is a decision we all have the ability to make.

Why *would* we want the Spirit to reside in us?

When we accept Christ and make Him Lord of our life, we aren't left to walk through the world blindly. We gain the Holy Spirit who becomes our compass and Counselor, our intercessor, our connection to Christ and the Father, and the power of God that we can call upon. The Spirit offers us understanding, truth, direction, and strength.

As a young person, my *compass* that I followed was always my parents, grandparents, teachers, and the laws I knew. Rules were instilled in me either by lesson or correction. I learned what these authority figures expected of me, and for the most part, I followed. But, little about what God expected of me was ever said.

When I was 12, I accepted Christ and was baptized. Of the three, I knew less about the Holy Spirit than I did about God and Jesus. That may be true of most people. As a young person, my ideas of a *spirit* were skewed by television programs and my own assumptions. The Holy Spirit was the hardest part for me as a child to understand about God.

I Corinthians 3:16 (NKJV) says, "Do you not know that you are the temple of God and that the Spirit of God dwells in you?"

I did not.

I was told, *The Holy Ghost lives in us.* How does He get there?

Why do I need the Holy Spirit? Don't I have Jesus?

How will I know He is guiding me, or if my direction is actually from me?

At first, I didn't have much help in understanding who the Holy Spirit is, and I spent much of my time focusing on the person of Jesus.

Once I started reading my Bible, however, and listening to others talk about the Spirit and praying on my own, I began connecting the dots. The One inside of me felt less like the angel on my shoulder and more like a friend in my thoughts and heart, who listened in my silence and put words to my feelings. I learned what it was to repent and how conviction felt.

I began understanding that Jesus had to die before the Holy Spirit came to stay. The Spirit has always existed and was part of creation (Genesis 1:2), but his permanent presence didn't come until Jesus' ascension (Acts 1:9).

It's still much for a mind to process–young or old–but once it does, once the connection is made, the Holy Spirit actually becomes the place inside us to turn.

April Motl also writes, "As we walk our journey of faith daily, more and more we learn to yield to the Holy Spirit in our thoughts, feelings, and actions, and as we do, we see God's glory and good poured out on our lives because we are learning how to live with God."[52]

Yielding is hard. It's a trust problem. A control problem for some. Count me in as a control person. But, little by little, I began yielding to the Holy Spirit.

So...

How *can* we receive the Holy Spirit?

- Make a confession of faith that Jesus is God's Son
- Declare Jesus arose from the dead and is seated at God's right hand
- Proclaim your decision to make Jesus the Lord of your life

Paul writes:

> "If you declare with your mouth, 'Jesus is Lord' and believe in your heart that God raised him from the dead, you will be saved." Romans 10:9-10 (my emphasis, NIV)

- Be baptized in the name of the Father, Son, and Holy Spirit

Jesus said to his disciples:

"All authority in heaven and on earth has been given to me. Therefore go and make disciples of all nations, baptizing them in the name of the Father and Son and the Holy Spirit and teaching them to obey everything I have commanded you. And surely I am with you always, to the very end of the age." Matthew 28:17-20 (NIV)

Jesus proclaims He is with us always, not in the form of a human, but as the Holy Spirit who moves in takes up residency within us!

I like the way April Motl states it: "The work God has for us to do and the work He has to accomplish in us for our good and His glory is part of the promise we receive **when the Holy Spirit comes into our hearts**."[60]

Using the Holy Spirit, God works in us and through us. For our good and His glory.

Next, comes understanding *why* we would want the Holy Spirit. In the disciples' ministry, after Jesus ascends, they are given gifts from the Holy Spirit to use. They are all sent out to spread the Word.

We are bestowed gifts as well…to go out and spread the Word. We can have one, or we can have many. Paul says,

"A spiritual gift is given to each of us so we can help each other. To one person the Spirit gives the ability **to give wise advice** to another the same Spirit gives a message of special **knowledge**. The same Spirit gives great **faith** to another, and to someone else the one Spirit gives **the gift of healing**. He gives one person the power **to perform miracles**, and another the ability **to prophesy**. He gives someone else the ability **to discern** whether a message is from the Spirit of God or from another spirit. Still another person is given the ability **to speak in unknown languages**, while another is given the ability **to interpret** what is being said. It is the one and only Spirit who distributes all these gifts. He alone decides which gift each person should have." I Corinthians 12:7-11(my emphasis, NLT)

A good friend asked me a long time ago if I had ever asked God to receive the gifts of the Spirit. I had never thought to. When she asked, I was honest. I told her that I was afraid. I didn't know if I was ready for such an important gifting. Remember, I said I was being honest.

I thought over that conversation for a long time. Finally, I told myself, *God knows me better than anyone. He knows if I am ready.*

I decided to trust Him, and I told Him so.

Courage comes with trust.

How are *you* with trusting someone? Is it hard to hand over the reins? Are you more comfortable being the one in charge? Do *you* fear the outcome won't be what you want?

When we fail or are hurt because someone lets us down, we become fearful to trust others. We hang onto the reins even more tightly. But, Jesus promises never to leave nor forsake us. Jesus promises to make our burdens easy and light if we yoke ourselves to Him.

It's taken time. Let go and lean into the Spirit. He becomes our intercessor–especially when an opportunity, decision, prayer, or suffering falls upon us. Ask Him to let you know what God's Will is for you. Ask Him to help you put into words what your pain or fear is. But, even if He doesn't, put your worries before Him. Ask that the door be wide open if a decision you face is God's will and shut it (in fact, slam it) if it's not. Then, wait.

As the late Tom Petty sings, *The waiting is the hardest part.*

How is the Spirit our connection to Christ?

Jesus knows what it is to be fully human. Yet, He is fully God as well. *Fully* means 100%. Fully human. Fully God. Now I know the math doesn't add up, but trust me on this.

Jesus faced temptation, pain, loss, and anger–all feelings of being human. But, unlike us, Jesus never sinned. Jesus is our example, our standard of living. He teaches us who the Father is and how we can live to honor the Father. Jesus teaches that He's come to save sinners and extoll grace rather than enforce the hundreds of laws created by church leaders. He teaches that He prefers mercy over the sacrifices that the leaders value.

Grace is a gift from God.

A story goes that C.S. Lewis was once asked, "What's unique about Christianity? That's easy," he said. "It's grace."[61] Grace is given by Jesus, and He gives it freely. No other faith in the world offers its followers that.

How else is the Spirit connecting us to Jesus?

Jesus sees all of the laws that the religious leaders have created. So, He simplifies them down to two: (Matthew 22:37-39 NIV)

- **"Love** the Lord your God with all your heart and with all your soul and with all your mind."

- "**Love** your neighbor as yourself"

If we "love"—as these words say–and if we ask the Spirit within us for help in loving, we will be as connected to Christ and each other as ever–because *God is love*. We will sound like Jesus, treat others like Jesus, be a light like Jesus, and forgive like Jesus.

The Holy Spirit is also a helper, an intercessor, who helps us in our weakness and prays for us when we can't for ourselves.

Paul tells us in Romans 8:26-27 (NIV) that in our pain, in our deep groanings, we may not know what we need or what to pray for.

We can call upon the Spirit to interpret these groanings, to put them into words, and to tell the Father exactly what we should lift up to him as a petition.

"And he who searches our heart knows the mind of the Spirit, because the Spirit intercedes for us."

Think of the most pain you've ever walked through. Physical pain, relationship pain, financial pain, depression, anxiety, fear. It hurts too much to even say words. It's like when you were a child, and you cried so hard that you couldn't even speak. You may not know what the exact issue is, or where to point your finger to the source. The Spirit can decide it, however. He can search your soul and your body for the source of your pain.

I suffered from diverticulitis for a period of time. Let me just say, *It is awful*. The first attack made me feel like I was dying. I felt I would explode inside. It was worse than all three of my kids' deliveries put together. In the ER, I cried out in pain for a long time. Nothing the staff gave me was helping. I rolled

135

on the table in agony. I screamed out for God's help, over and over again.

"God, help me! God, help me!"

Before too long, I felt something "break". My screaming became a moan. The pain began leveling out. Was I dying? At least the pain would be over.

It wasn't that the medicine finally started working.

I was exhausted, but I also felt a peace wash over me.

That's just a physical example that I could share. Like most people, I have had my share of financial and relationship pain, anxiety, and fear. The power of the Holy Spirit can intercede for our pain as well as use us for someone else's.

In Ephesians 3:14-21, Paul said that he prays that the Father deeply strengthens his people with **power** through his Spirit, and he prays that we, as a body of believers, have the **power** to comprehend just how much God really loves us.

This power is not magic. It's not to entertain or be a show. Any power or gifts we may be given are not to elevate us, but to glorify God. If we use our God-given gifts of the Spirit, we will be better prepared for what is to come and in our daily walk.

In Acts I, scripture refers to the Holy Spirit and his power in several different ways. Read Acts I and II if you want the full context.

- Jesus gave instructions *through the Holy Spirit.* (Verse 2)
- Jesus called the Spirit *the gift my Father prom-ised.* (Verse 4)
- You will be *baptized by the Holy Spirit.* (Verse 5)
- You will *receive power when the Holy Spirit comes to you.* (Verse 8)

- The Holy Spirit *spoke through David* about Judas. (Verse 16)

In Acts 2, the Holy Spirit came upon Jesus' disciples in different forms.

- like the *sound of a violent blowing wind* (Verse 2)
- *like tongues of fire* that separated and rested upon each of them (Verse 3)
- *in other tongues* as the Spirit enabled them (Verse 4)
- young men will have *visions*, old men will dream *dreams*, and servants will experience *prophecies* (Verses 14-21)

Who God is, who Jesus is, and who the Holy Spirit is continue to be revealed to us as our relationship with the three grows.

Earlier, Paul told us we are God's house and the temple of the living God. That we are built by God and all glory goes to Him, the builder. However, we are like that empty house in Southeast Indiana–vacant and without power–**unless** we let the Holy Spirit in.

That is what we were built for. *That* is who really owns us. And, *that* is where we find courage, strength, and power–the Holy Spirit who indwells us.

I invite you to say this prayer with me:

Heavenly Father, As I drive past homes–empty for whatever reason–may I think of the potential each place has. People will most likely move in, but my prayer is that YOU move in as well. May the family and their home become a light for the neighborhood and community. May the children have an influence over those in their schools. May You be worshiped and a strong presence in that place.

You ARE the "builder of everything." May I be a good steward of what you have given me and made me to be. Keep my body and home safe and healthy. I invite you into both.

Make me courageous, trusting in Your Will, and may Your Spirit come to dwell in my heart because I accept Jesus as my Lord and Savior. I receive Your gifts of the Spirit and devote myself and my life to glorifying You. Amen

Application: Anointing

Many who have done mission work have never seen a dedication. They've served on dozens of trips, but never seen one completed. We were blessed to attend two dedications in one day!

After tornadoes had wreaked havoc on Tuscaloosa, Alabama, in 2011, the carnage was cleared and rebuilding started. Samaritan's Purse was just one ministry to help homeowners repair or start over. My husband Mark, our daughter Mari, and I went with a group from our church.

The day we arrived, we learned two homes would be finished the week that we were there. We were ecstatic! I had seen pictures and heard about them, but we were going to witness it for ourselves…twice!

Both dedications were similar, but unique. The energy was so high, preparing for them. The words spoken and presentations were similar, but the families were unique. The homes were unique. Their experiences in the storm were unique.

Miss Violet lived and stood alone, but not in volunteers or Spirit.

Mrs. Beverly had her immediate family with her and a beautiful glow about her, too.

Each was handed an invoice marked "Paid in Full" and a Bible signed by those who worked on her home. Each was given a set of keys, and a plaque marked their front door.

Earlier in the week, while I worked in Miss Violet's bathroom, she sat on the side of her bed and began talking. I don't think she actually was conversing with me so much as she was vocally unwinding her thoughts. Maybe they were groanings, as Paul said earlier.

"Why, all these people came from all over, you know. Came to help me?" she said. "Isn't that somethin'?"

I was on the floor and I turned to her. "I heard about the trip, and I just felt something inside say that I was supposed to be here." I paused. "I think that's why all of us are here."

That, for me, is how the Holy Spirit works. I feel something stirring inside. I listen. And, I pray.

I believe God selects what He wants us to hear. There are calls for help going up everywhere, every day. Maybe a call for help, like in Tuscaloosa. The Spirit may lead us into foreign territory. I had never been to Tuscaloosa before, much less thought about it.

The Spirit has a tendency to call me to love on strangers, in all of their hurting, and serve them.

Miss Violet, in her beautiful smile and pearl necklace, cried a lot that week. She praised God and thanked Him. She hugged strangers, and she joined us all in anointing her new home.

Miss Violet and Mrs. Washington not only opened up their residential homes to us, but I believe their spiritual ones, too— the one in their heart and soul. Volunteers joined both women in praying for and anointing their homes with oil.

To *anoint* means to cover in blessing and to dedicate to the Lord. Dabbing oil on doors, furniture, rooms, and walls and committing them to what is pleasing and glorifying to God is an anointing.

Pastor and author Tony Evans says, "Every Christian has *the anointing*. If you are saved, you have it. You possess it. You own it. It is there."[62]

So, first can you say, "I am saved!"?

Can you answer with certainty?

Evans explains, "The anointing is the indwelling presence of the Holy Spirit, designed to do his work, in your life."[63]

Read Exodus 40:1-38.

When the Tabernacle is complete, worshiping should be able to commence. However, it's just a tent unless God fills the place with his Spirit.

What does God command Moses to anoint in Exodus 40?

_____ _____
_____ _____
_____ _____
_____ _____
_____ _____

Could we not do the same with our home?

What could you anoint in your home–to cover in blessing and dedicate to the Lord?

_____ _____
_____ _____
_____ _____
_____ _____

Each year, the Sunday before the school year began, a group of teachers and staff where I taught walked the hallways at school. We prayed together; we prayed as we walked alone; we anointed the lockers, classroom doors, desks, and walls. We wanted the Holy Spirit's presence in our school and with us and our students.

Do you see, we can invite the Holy Spirit into any place we go?

Could we not go throughout our community, anointing places we want the Lord to be invited in, to cover with blessing, and to protect and provide?

Absolutely.

The enemy would love nothing better than to try to work his way into our lives and to plant himself into our homes, our schools, and our communities. We need to know that's how he operates.

Write Joshua 24:15 on the lines below:

_____

_____

Whether you have that verse on the wall in your home or the walls of your heart, let the Lord take up residency in you. Let the gift of the Holy Spirit lead you and use you. Not for your glory, but for His. Trust the Spirit. Be courageous. Be a light.

Wherever you are, you are God's house. Serve Him well.

Photo by Mark Bennett
On a walk in Prairieton, Indiana–2022

Chapter Eleven

A House of Refuge

"Come, behold the works of the Lord"
Psalm 46:8 (NKJV)

*R*adar, satellites, and cameras detect and record storms on the surface and from the air. Meteorologists look at the damage and determine the severity of the storm using the Enhanced Fujita (EF) scale. They can measure wind speeds and assess the debris field. But, what they can't see or measure is how a storm harms someone on the inside.

But, God can.

Many events in our life can devastate us and leave everything in total chaos. Events like losing a job. Or, losing a family member. Seeing your child struggle. Watching your spouse walk away, taking your heart with them. Loving someone who is being destroyed by an addiction.

In earlier chapters, we looked at all the ways God has shielded us from the enemy's schemes. We know that God has plans for us, to prosper us and not harm us. He not only told this to his people captive in Babylon, but He speaks it to us as well.

God has established a firm foundation through the prophets, Jesus, and his disciples. God gave that foundation to Moses in the law, but also to us in the commands Jesus gave us–to love God with all our heart, soul, and mind and to love our neighbors as ourselves.

God makes himself our stronghold, a safe place. His protective walls keep out what might want to harm us. Nehemiah built walls around Jerusalem, and God's boundaries are for us, too. These parameters aren't meant to keep us captive but safe.

The same God who protects us with walls can tear down others that He wants to free us from. The walls of Jericho came down because God wanted them down. If a wall isn't from Him, then let's tell the Lord to remove it and clear the way.

Earlier, we looked at the parable Jesus told in connecting ourselves–like a branch to the vine–to the power of Christ. On our own, we may not realize all that we were created for and the strength and gifts the Spirit gives us. But with Christ, we can defeat giants with God-given courage and power. We have inside of us the same power that rose Jesus from the grave.

Scripture says man concerns himself with outward appearances, but God is more concerned with the heart. The facade we spend so much time focusing on isn't where our attention should be. It should be on the Holy Spirit who indwells us. That light is meant to be a beacon, calling people to the Christ they see in us, not what we are wearing or how we appear.

God is our place of refuge and tenant. He not only built a place *for us*, but *in us*. He is in both. The One who builds everything, who offers himself *to us*, has also turned us into a home, a temple for the Holy Spirit who will permanently dwell *in us* once we accept Jesus as our Lord.

146

This book that you hold in your hands is for me as well as it is for you. I need God. I battle fear. I face trouble. Though I have accepted Christ and talk to Him about my weaknesses and though I lean into Him for strength, I live in this broken world, too. I battle thoughts and feelings. That's why I ask God to search my heart and test my thoughts for anything that holds me back.

I am a work in progress, and so are you.

Let's spend our last chapter together looking at Psalm 46 to understand what the psalmist proclaims about God. It's what I have been saying to you from the beginning. Verse 1 says:

> God *is* our refuge and strength,
> A very present help in trouble."

God has proven time and time again that He is with us. He *is present in* our circumstances. God doesn't come to us after we walk *into trouble*. He is with us before, during, and after–and He *helps* us. Not to get what we want, but to help us get through the circumstances we are in.

In Daniel 3, Shadrach, Meshach, and Abednego are about to be thrown into the fiery furnace of Babylon's king because they refuse to bow down to him. In their trouble, the three vow to the king that their God will deliver them if they are put into the fire. They get their *strength* from the Lord. They say to Nebuchadnezzar that their God will save them from the fire and from the king. He will be their *refuge*. The Lord they have worshiped will save them from the fire, while they are in the fire, or if they die, deliver them from the fire into his hands.

God not only *helps* them in the fire, but He is also *very present* with them in it.

Nebuchadnezzar exclaims, "Look! I see four men walking around in the fire, unbound and unharmed, and the fourth looks like the son of the gods" (Daniel 3:25 NIV).

The three–Shadrach, Meshach, and Abednego–are joined by a fourth man, "like the son of the gods." Jesus is with them in their *trouble* just as He is in ours.

Verse 2 says:

"Therefore we will not fear"

Fear is a natural human emotion. It's programmed into our nervous system. *Fear* can activate a survival instinct that can keep us safe when facing danger.[64]

Jesus who is fully God is also fully Man. Jesus faced temptation as well as fear.

After the Last Supper, Jesus goes to the Garden of Gethsemane to pray. He knows his time on earth is near the end. He asks Peter, James, and John to stay with Him, keep watch with Him, and pray. Fully-man Jesus asks his closest disciples to stay near.

Jesus' arrest is coming. He is sorrowful and troubled. Jesus tells them, "My soul is overwhelmed with sorrow to the point of death" (Matthew 26:36-38 NIV).

Jesus is fearful. Sorrowful. Troubled.

He prays to his Father asking if his death really has to happen this way. Jesus prays this three times. He asks the same question: "May this cup [of God's wrath] be taken from me?"

How many times have we prayed, *God, will you take this away from me?*

Jesus' fear is intense. Peter, James, and John don't help Him. In fact, they fail Him. All three fall asleep when He needs their prayer and attention. God answers Jesus' prayer but not the Way Jesus hopes.

How many times has the answer to our prayers not been what we asked for?

The law is on its way to arrest Jesus. His fear is so severe that He even sweats blood (Luke 22:44).

Though Jesus is Son of Man, He is also Son of God. Jesus knows God's plan is to save the world, and it can only be done at the cost of Jesus' life. Sinless Jesus. Jesus surrenders his physical well-being for our eternal one.

We may or may not know what God's purpose is for us, but it doesn't mean his plan isn't to be for our well-being or someone else's.

When fear becomes irrational and creates intense anxiety for us, experts say we should seek help from a general practitioner, a psychologist, or a counselor.[65] We need help. Intense levels of anxiety and stress are harmful.

Our Father in heaven *is* Doctor and Mighty Counselor. That's whom Jesus turns to. The strength He needs to endure the persecution He is about to face can only come from the Father.

We can consult God's counsel in scripture and prayer, too. God's Word tells us that

- He will deliver us from our fears (Psalm 34:4)
- He is with us wherever we go (Joshua 1:9)
- The Holy Spirit inside of us is a Spirit of power and love and self-control and not fear (2 Timothy 1:6-7)
- Our hearts are not meant to be troubled (John 14:27)

- The Lord is our light and salvation; we have all that we need (Psalm 27:1)
- Whoever trusts in the Lord is safe (Proverbs 29:25)

Jesus experiences natural fear but submits to his Heavenly Father's authority and his Father's will. Jesus could have stopped his arrest and come down off of the cross, but He surrenders to his Father's plans. Jesus knows He will die, be buried, and three days later rise again. In fact, He has told his disciples so. This claim is part of what got Him crucified–claiming the "temple" would be destroyed and three days later restored. Jesus knows He will ascend to heaven and sit at the right hand of his Father. But, He has to suffer first.

Because Jesus died on the cross for our sins, because He rose from the grave. God's answer to our most crucial prayer has already been given–we can know the Father, through his Son, and live this life with both living in us as the Holy Spirit. This answered prayer means we can have a relationship with Him now as we await eternity with Him in the future.

Verses 2-3 of Psalm 46 read:

> "Even though the earth be removed,
> And though the mountains be carried into
> the midst of the sea;
>
> *Though* its waters roar *and* be troubled,
> Though the mountains shake with its swelling."

Serving on disaster relief teams for several years, my family has seen what floods, tornadoes, and hurricanes are capable of.

EF 3 winds peel roofs as if they were aluminum foil. Trees fall and crush homes and cars. Houses wash away in flash flooding like toys floating in a bathtub. Mud fills houses and buries cars. Hurricanes do all of these. Verses 2-3 says even if the world experiences the absolute worst of cataclysmic events, as in:

- the earth being destroyed
- the mountains are broken and washed into the sea
- the flood waters rage
- and, the mountains are rattled

we will not fear.

Winds and rain aren't the only cataclysmic events of life. Storms of divorce and separation severely damage and destroy marriages. Bankruptcy, illness, and death of a loved one wreck us to our very soul. There's loss. Mourning. Salvaging whatever is left means picking up fractured pieces of life. Saving the kids. Holding onto our mutual friendships. Challenges come from what he said and what she said. Rebuilding lives needs courage and strength...and forgiveness. No disaster agency or relief organization can comfort us like the arms of the Father.

The psalmist recognizes again and again that hardships of all types hammer at us. *Though* this happens and *though* that, he brings us the comforting news...God is! And, we need not fear.

Psalm 46:4-5 tells us:

> *There is* a river whose streams shall make glad
> the city of God,
> The holy *place* of the tabernacle of the Most High

> God *is* in the midst of her, she shall not be moved;
> God shall help her, just at the break of dawn.

Though a roaring river can wash away homes and roads in its path and *though* a hurricane can blow businesses and schools off of their foundations, one river that we can rejoice and be *glad in* is the river of Living Water that flows from Christ. Every little *stream* from this river is a blessing. This is one river that is not a threat, but a gift.

The apostle John says the vision God has given him of "heaven," or the New Jerusalem or Eden, has a river running through the middle of the streets. The river flows from the thrones of God and "the Lamb". They are the river's source, and it waters the very Tree of Life that we once lost access to through Adam. But, not anymore. We will live in God's presence forever (Revelation 22).

In John 4, Jesus talks with the Samaritan woman at the well. He tells her that men will always continue to ask for water from a well because they physically get thirsty. However, if they would approach Jesus and ask for the *living water* He offers, men would spiritually be satisfied and never want for anything.

In John 7, Jesus tells those who want to be His followers to *Come!* Drink from the *living water* that He offers, and they will receive the Holy Spirit when Jesus comes into His glory.

Water has healing powers–physically and spiritually.

Verse 6 of Psalms 46 tell us what may become of this world:

> The nations raged, the kingdoms were moved;
> He uttered His voice, the earth melted.

Especially in the days since the COVID-19 pandemic, I don't think anyone would disagree that the turmoil in the world has escalated and created more division. Nations and kingdoms rage on. Racial injustice cries out for change. Nations choose sides in a fight for control of land and resources that each claims belongs to them. People die. Rage flares over gun violence versus gun rights. Protests over identity, rights, and choice. While the world rages on, God softly speaks, He *utters*, and one day, all that we fight over will be gone. Nations, kingdoms, races, guns, and death.

However, in verse 7, the psalmist consoles us:

> The LORD of hosts *is* with us;
> The God of Jacob *is* our refuge.

In an earlier chapter, I mentioned the empty house that sat vacant for more than 20 years. The beautiful, two-story home that has not been lived in. We, too, can sit empty, like that beautiful home near the highway. Everyone drives by wondering what's to become of it. However, the Lord wants to dwell in us. To move in permanently. We are reminded that He is not only the Lord but also in charge of the whole universe. He is the *Lord of hosts*. That means, Lord of all angels and armies. God who is with us offers us protection and comfort.

> Come, behold the works of the LORD,
> Who has made desolations in the earth.
> He makes wars cease to the end of the earth;
>
> He breaks the bow and cuts the spear in two;
> He burns the chariot in the fire.

What can our God do for us? Come and look! Behold the works of the Lord. He can bring to ruin anything that comes against us. God can destroy those who want to see us hurt. Wars and bow, spear and chariot are all controlled and directed by his hand. Whatever way the enemy may try to attack us, God makes, breaks, and burns Satan's weapons. Peace that doesn't seem possible, is possible.

The fighting between family members, fights that seem irreconcilable, can be restored with God's hands. A politically divided nation can unite when God softens hearts. Lands that have been ravaged by war or drought can become fruitful and safe if his hands pour out peace upon the people. The illness that threatens may take our life but not our salvation.

So many prayers for peace pour out for nations and people every day. God hears each and every prayer, and they won't go unanswered. So, let's continue praying that soon, God reconciles and restores so children and families can be safe and live in peace.

Some of the psalmist's most renown words are in Verse 10:

> Be still, and know that I *am* God;
> I will be exalted among the nations,
> I will be exalted in the earth!

All of the other verses in Psalm 46 are in third person. The psalmist speaks. In this verse, God is the one speaking. What God is commanding is an imperative: *Be still, and know that I am God*. It's not a question. God doesn't tell us that we have to search for Him to find Him. We don't have to *work* to discover Him. The *I-Am God* is! If we would just stop our fighting and contesting God, put down our fists and weapons to surrender and acknowledge *He is God*. Know that He is God. It's then, and most of all, we can discover God right where we are.

The prophet Elijah felt so alone. All the rest of God's prophets had been killed. Elijah was the only prophet left. He zealously sought the Lord. Standing on Horeb, the mountain of God, the Lord passed by Elijah. A strong wind tore through the mountains and broke rocks into pieces. Then, an earthquake erupted. Finally, a great fire grew. Could any battle or storm be greater than these? In winds and earthquakes and fires, the Lord did not speak. It was in a small whisper that the Lord spoke.

Listening for the soft, small voice of God means we must surrender ourselves to hear Him. Not being vexatious. Not monopolizing the conversation. If we quiet down and lean in, we may hear what He has to say to us. God *can* expound with a powerful booming voice from the mountaintops. It just may be that in our circumstances God may have us looking for and listening to who He is and what He is saying.

In Mark 4, Jesus is in a boat on the way to the other side of the Sea of Galilee. It was becoming evening, and Jesus began resting in the stern of the boat. Wind speeds suddenly increased and waves started breaking over the sides, filling the boat with water. Jesus continued to sleep.

His disciples woke Him, asking, "Teacher, don't you care if we drown?"

Jesus commanded the wind and waves to "Quiet! Be still!" and they did (Verses 38-39).

The same words He said in Psalm 46:10, He speaks to us and the disciples in the storm. The wind and the waves recognize Jesus' authority, and we are called to do so as well.

The disciples in the boat ask each other, "Who is this?"

In Psalm 46:10, in our circumstances–in the illness, in the bankruptcy, in the abandonment–we can know it is God who is with us. He is *in* the boat. He isn't waiting for us to come to him. He isn't waiting until your circumstances are over to see if you'll make it through. The Lord is attentive to us and has authority over the situation.

He is speaking to you and me.

Know that I am God. Know that I am present. Know that I have authority over the situation. Know that you can hear from Me if you lean in.

Verse 11 repeats:

> The LORD of hosts *is* with us;
> The God of Jacob *is* our refuge."

The Lord in his authority brings power into our situation and tells us not to fear what we are experiencing but to concentrate on who He is. The God of Jacob.

Why Jacob? Why add Jacob to the earlier verse, "God is our refuge"?

The battles of Jacob were known by his people. God knew the battles, too. Jacob battled fear and anxiety. God knew how he felt. Jacob feared his brother Esau had come to kill him (for taking his birthright from him). God knew what he did. Jacob went to the Lord, "Save me, I pray" (Genesis 32:11 NIV). God heard his prayer. He knew it all. The stories of Jacob were known by God's people, and the stories of you and me are known by God, too. Our battles, our feelings, what we've done, and especially our prayers.

Like Jacob, many of us know the feeling of loneliness and running for our life. Jacob struggled not only with humans but also with God.

How about you? Are you struggling with other people? How about God? Are you struggling with God right now?

We keep saying God is our refuge. But, He isn't a building with cinder block walls, alarm systems, and a basement. God doesn't protect us with bars over the windows. Our Father is a refuge of unending empathy and forgiveness. He is a strong soldier and a compassionate friend. God is present in our joy and sorrow. Our Father is always ready to listen. God leads us and carries us.

What God was then, He is now, and He always will be.

God was a refuge for Noah and his family when the floods consumed everyone else. God passed over his people in Egypt and protected them as others died from the plague. God protected Daniel from the mouths of lions. Don't think that the God of heaven hasn't got your name written on the palm of his hand. He has rescued us who call Him Lord and Father from the death that sin brings. Nothing we do will keep Him from watching over us. Nothing.

Say that to yourself over and over, *Therefore, we need not fear.* I will say it with you.

Therefore, we need not fear.

I encourage you to listen to "Psalm 46 (Lord of Hosts)" by Capital City Music before we end this time together. Let the Word of God put to song be a time of worship for you.

I invite you to join me in this prayer:

Heavenly Father, Sometimes, just a thought takes my peace from me. I focus on the storm of my circumstances. I particularly worry (about ...) even days later. The storms can be over, but my anxiety is not. Lord, may your Word remind me of the ways You have rescued those before me. Help me see how You are with me. I ask for strength now. Strength from You. Help me take my thoughts captive when I see they make me anxious and fearful.

Psalm 46 tells me that You are a very present help in trouble. I'm just going to say it: Lord, please end the wars that I battle. Break the bow and spears that try to attack me.

Quiet my mind as I focus on Your presence.

Make my heart Your throne. Yet, I will praise you all the days of my life. Amen

Application: A House of Prayer

Emily is a fiber artist. She creates some of the most colorful, imaginative pieces–big and small. One particular installation involved her entire church.

Emily isn't shy around construction tools. She can design, weld, and assemble materials of all sorts. This project encompassed designing a "house" of wood, brackets, screws, and string.

Angles were pieced together, the lumber was painted, and holes were drilled for the string. "Walls" were created using parallel lines of string running vertically. Light was easily able to permeate through the openings. What Emily wanted others to add to her work was the Spirit.

Photo by Emily Bennett
Maryland Community Church–2016

To see this creation become what Emily planned, she invited members of the church to write a prayer, Bible verse, or drawing on a strip of paper and then weave it in the walls or ceiling of the structure. Young and old, parents and their children, were eager to be involved.

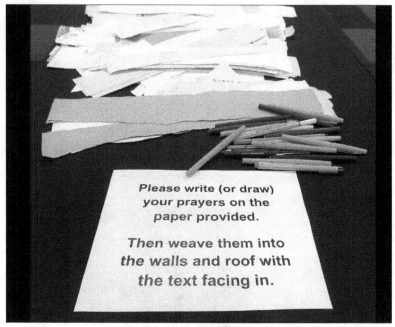

Photo by Emily Bennett
Maryland Community Church–2016

Helpers stepped in to weave prayers in the ceiling and high on the walls. The various colors created a beautiful, organized mosaic. Different handwritings, drawings, colorful lettering–enclosed the house and gave it a unique character.

Photo by Emily Bennett
Maryland Community Church–2016

Prayer House is its name. Fitting for its shape but also its walls of individual requests and praises. Seeing the walls and ceiling filled made entering the room a private and personal experience. What you could once see outside of the house was now closed off to you. The installation is not a large piece. Perfect for one person, yet open, and not so small to make someone claustrophobic.

Photo by Emily Bennett
Maryland Community Church–2016

Standing in *Prayer House,* my eyes wandered from prayer to prayer to prayer, causing me to look up to read prayers on the "ceiling." It filled me with such a feeling of peace and contentment. All that love and grace enveloped me. It felt safe. It was a Spirit-filled place.

A few weeks later at another showing, I was blessed to stand back and watch students experience *Prayer House* the way I had. The way Emily had envisioned.

There was an opening which clearly identified the way in and out, but once inside, students didn't step in and step out quickly. They couldn't possibly read all of the prayers, but they sure tried.

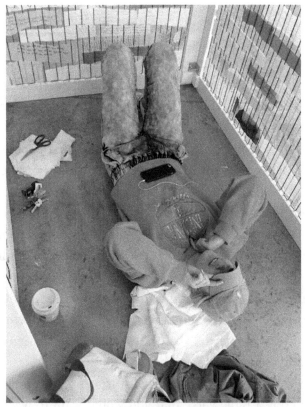

Photo by Emily Bennett
Maryland Community Church–2016

Students made themselves comfortable. They reclined, knelt, and stood. Some made simple furniture out of their backpacks. Clearly many hands went into this project. Some students even wanted to add their own prayers to what already existed.

We have seen in this study that God is the builder of everything. He planned this world and all of us. He built it, and then… He built us. God breathed life into each one of us and has made a way for us to connect to him through his Son Jesus Christ.

God, our refuge, is not what we turn to but who. He is Creator, builder, our protector, our source of power. He is Light and Spirit. God has been our refuge in scripture–giving us the foundations of the law, the walls to guard us from evil and attack, and the Holy Spirit's company in our times of trouble and prayer.

Part of *Prayer House* that I love most is that people write on paper what's in their heart, and that message becomes part of the house. Without prayer, the house isn't realizing its creator's purpose. Without prayer, it isn't sharing the Gospel with others. A house filled with prayer seems to be soaked in Spiritual goodness, love, and security. One without prayer seems like an empty shell.

I'm a big fan of keeping a journal. I've done it for years. I write what I want to remember, what I've discovered, and prayers I want to revisit. I write how I share my experience with others and connect them to the God I know.

The last task I have for you is to write a prayer, draw a picture, or copy a Bible verse that you would want to weave into the *Prayer House* installation yourself:

Now, do this today and tomorrow. Put these around your home and fill your refuge with words that embrace and comfort you. Share them with others. Revisit them. Start your day with a new strip of paper.

Make this a daily habit to connect to the power source you have dwelling inside of you. I know this lifts anxiety and stress. I have experienced it myself. Your car can be your refuge. A closet or spare room can become your *Prayer House*. A jog down a country road or taking a seat in a coffee shop booth. Light breaks through when you pray–whether your eyes are open or closed, palms together or on a steering wheel. The same Light of Christ that attracts you will attract those who see Him in you.

Share what you have learned with others. Tell them that they do not need to struggle alone. A quiet house does not mean an empty house, if you have the Spirit of Christ within you.

Conclusion: But Until Then...

At the end of a vacation as we pull into the driveway, I always seem to take a deep breath and exhale. It feels good to be home. It's a relief to walk in the back door, to familiar surroundings, and to sleep in my own bed.

There's something therapeutic about being home.

God wants you to come home. To take a deep breath, feel welcome, and be relieved to be in familiar surroundings. He offers that to you in His refuge.

Recently, I spoke with my friend Rebekah Price. Her heart has always been to care for others. Rebekah has served with the Mercy Ships, as a surgical nurse, helping those who wouldn't get medical care without this mission partner. Rebekah's work and continued study has taken her many places, and she's served patients in the toughest, but sometimes most beautiful, season of their life. Their dying days.

Having witnessed Hospice care with my father-in-law and seeing my grandma's last days in the nursing home, I understand just a little of what end-of-life care looks like. Rebekah has spent her most recent years caring for patients in their last months, weeks, and hours.

Rebekah says an overwhelming majority of her patients want to die at home. My father-in-law was able to go home before his passing. His family cared for him for three weeks. My grandmother, however, was not able to go home. I could definitely see the difference in their care and comfort level where they were.

Rebekah Price says often the patient's bed is set up in the living room or dining room if it is possible. A more spacious, central location in the home than a bedroom in the back of a house. The living room and dining room are more of a place of activity in the home and hold some of the dearest memories for the patient. Rebekah also says it's common for the patient's bed to be near *light* or beside a window.

Being at home, in a room filled with love and activity, and near light can bring the patient joy and comfort. That's what hospice care is about–*optimally* providing medical care and comfort to patients in their own home, familiar surroundings around them, and people with them whom they may recognize with them.

In the precious time Rebekah Price has spent with her patients, she says she often learns what means the most to those she's caring for.

She hears about her patients' experiences and travels but what they mostly talk about are relationships, Rebekah says. She hears about family–husbands, wives, children and grandchildren. Her patients also talk about their regrets. Some patients tell her what they wish they had done and never did. Most often though, Rebekah says her patients want to talk about loved ones–family and friends.

Reflecting on these conversations, Rebekah says that we work so hard to build up assets and account balances, but in the process, we may miss what's most valuable in our lives–our relationships.

Here on Earth, our homes are just brick and mortar. Rust and moths will one day destroy them, or (like King Solomon said in Ecclesiastes) we'll leave them behind for someone else to enjoy.

For hospice patients, going home can be comforting and less stressful, not because their house is worth a large sum of money, but because of the love and memories that seem embedded in the home. Memories on the walls, flashbacks around the table, giggles from years ago, echoing from the playroom, and conversations between loved ones. Those are what is valuable.

My prayer is this book changes your way of seeing the home that God has built for you and me–here and in Heaven. One is temporary. The other is eternal.

I've lived in many different homes in my lifetime. I'm sure you've had several yourself. But, once we leave this earthly place, we will come into our *final* home, and we will never say *goodbye* again.

But, until then…

We have a choice if that eternal home is going to be spent *with* Jesus or *without* Him. Our decision *now,* will determine which it will be.

Choosing to become a follower of Jesus *now* assures us that when the day comes, we will join him in our new home–free of darkness, illness, poverty, storms, and death. Until then, we can have a life abundant in God's love, a relationship full of grace and mercy, and a place to turn in our fear, grief, and pain.

Heaven will not be a refuge. We won't need to flee from anyone or anything. Heaven will be empty of all that. Heaven will be absent of all that we fear.

But, until that time, why not live in the shelter of the Lord? Why not tuck yourself up under his wing?

I ask you, *Who is Jesus to you?*

Do you see Him for who He is–the Son of God?

Do you know what He has done for you–died on a cross for your sins and mine?

Do you understand his promises–to protect and provide for you here on earth while he is preparing a place for you in Heaven?

And, don't you want to enjoy a relationship with him *now*? You can through the Holy Spirit.

When we accept Jesus as our Lord and Savior, we receive the Holy Spirit. We can trust Him. We will have everything we need.

Jesus is our foundation, our protection, our source of power and our light. John 15:4 says that Jesus abides in his children and we in Him. The Holy Spirit that He has given us is our compass and counselor.

As you look around where you live now, my prayer is that you feel the presence of the Lord. That the walls remind you of the protection you've been given in the Lord.

Occasionally, we experience our electricity going out. Sometimes, it can be off for days. In the darkness, we can have such a hard time seeing and making our way through a room. We tend to look out the windows to see if others around us have power. Nearly everything we use or do seems to need power and light. We've become dependent on electricity, making it hard to go without it.

In John 8:12 (NIV), "When Jesus spoke again to the people, he said 'I am the light of the world. **Whoever follows me will never walk in darkness**, but will have the light of life'" (my emphasis).

The choice to follow Jesus is yours. Don't wait. Tell someone today that you want to have a relationship with Jesus. You will not regret it. God is not keeping anyone from his power. He's just waiting for the invitation into your life.

God has a plan for you, and all has been prepared. During the time you spend on this earth, God promises to be your refuge and strength, even when the mountains shake. He wants to be your safe place.

The Author

*T*eri Bennett taught more than thirty-five years of secondary and post-graduate education and found her niche working with middle school students. Since retiring from the classroom, Teri continues to lead Bible study groups with her husband, speaks to women's groups, serves on disaster relief teams, and facilitates high school students in entrepreneurial exploration. One of her greatest loves, however, is writing about Christ.

Getting closer to Christ by digging into scripture has become Teri's biggest personal commitment. The book you hold in your hands is just one particular study.

Teri and her husband Mark live in Indiana near the families of their grown children–Graham, Paul, and Mari. Teri and Mark enjoy treasure hunting in used book stores and thrift shops, reading in coffee shops, and traveling. Teri and Mark have greatly influenced each other's work as writers and educators.

Mission work touches Teri's heart deeply and takes her to many places she's never been. The bonds established between her, the other volunteers, and homeowners are priceless to her. Teri's eyes are always on that next place God is calling her to go.

Acknowledgements

*F*or the past year, whenever I would ask my husband Mark what he wanted to do for the day, he knew in my heart I wanted to go to Java Haute Coffee Co. and write. I had this book on my mind all of the time. I just wanted to get my thoughts on paper.

Mark has always supported and taken interest in my teaching, writing, and faith walk. He and our kids–Graham, Paul, and Mari–are encouragement and great examples of chasing what God calls us to do. Thank you to them and Kristy, Emily, and Kyle; I love you like you are my own.

I'm so thankful I could retire early from teaching. This past year has been wonderful for my soul. A true transition. I've spent more time with our grandkids, volunteered in several places, and connected with my parents. What a gift this season has been. I've had more time to think, finish this book, and talk to God.

Pete and Connie Massa have been a wonderful first audience for this book. Real friends read rough drafts.

Amy Barbour has been more than just a test audience, too. She has been a friend whom I've kept in mind as I wrote. She's been my Plus-One for a long time. I encourage her, and she encourages me.

Thank you, Java Haute Coffee Co., for keeping the lattes hot.

We never know how something we say or teach may plant a seed. Pastor Doug Napier of Maryland Community Church, I'm sure, had no idea a sermon he gave way back when, on God being our refuge, would take root in me. We sat down and talked more about it afterwards. I took notes. Keep doing what God has you doing, Doug.

I want to say, "Thank you, Lord, for bringing Samaritan's Purse into my life." It has been a blessing to me in ways that I try to share with people who will listen. My faith walk made great strides when I said *yes* to serving on a team in 2010 with Mark, daughter Mari, and 10 special people from our church. I have seen what your mission is, Samaritan's Purse, how God calls us to step in and serve, and how blessings pour out to homeowners, volunteers, the hosting church, and the community.

I can't say enough about how this book has been a step out of my comfort zone. I am not a *builder* the way our world would define it. But, *Kingdom builder* might fit me a little better. Rick Warren says a Kingdom builder draws wisdom and truth found only in the Bible. A Kingdom builder takes guidance from the Holy Spirit. And, a Kingdom builder gathers with other Kingdom builders for encouragement and accountability.[66] Those three things have brought me peace and blessings.

Bibliography

"5 challenges faced while building Dubai's Burj Khalifa." *Khaleej Times.* Accessed January 4, 2019. https://www. khaleejtimes.com/uae/5-challenges-faced-while-building-dubais-burj-khalifa.

"About Coast Redwoods." *California Department of Parks and Recreation.* Accessed January 6, 2020. https://www.parks. ca.gov/?page_id=22257.

"Andrea Bocelli Talks About His Strong Faith in God." *EWTN News In-Depth.* Youtube. April 10, 2021. Video, 11:13. https://youtu.be/oN_FVhfZEPw.

"Andrew Ripp–Jericho (Acoustic)" YouTube. January 10, 2021. Video, 2:19. https://www.youtube.com/ watch?v=qb9B__C55aA).

Bendix, Mark. "Electrical Design for Tall Buildings." *Consulting–Specifying Engineer.* August 1, 2007. https://www.csemag.com/articles/ electrical-design-for-tall-buildings/.

"Break Tests or Maturity Method?" *Maturix*, March 11, 2021. https://maturix.com/knowledge-center/break-tests-vs-maturity-method.

"Casting Crowns–Just Be Held (Live)." YouTube. January 27, 2016. Video, 3:43. https://www.youtube.com/watch?v=s53R3aj5pfc.

Clawson, David Roger M.D. "What You Need to Know About Spiritual Illness and Disease." *Psychology Today.* March 20, 2021. https://www.psychology-today.com/sg/blog/deconstructing-illness/202103/what-you-need-know-about-spiritual-illness-and-disease.

Collins, Craig. "The Overview Effect." *Issuu.* Accessed March 6, 2023. https://issuu.com/faircountmedia/docs/international_20space_20station_2020_20years_20of_/s/11253985.

Conscius, Jura. "How to furnish, fill and decorate your new, larger home." *Washington Post.* September 21, 2021. https://www.washingtonpost.com/home/2021/09/21/how-to-furnish-decorate-upsize-home.

Craven, Jackie. "Safe Rooms and Shelters–What You Need to Know." *ThoughtCo.* September 25, 2018. https://www.thoughtco.com/safe-room-what-is-a-safe-room-177327.

"Danny Gokey–Stay Strong (Official Music Video)." YouTube. February 10, 2023. Video, 3:18. https://www.youtube.com/watch?v=TY-jh4RS_I0.

"Durability: The Cornerstone of Sustainable Construction!" *Cortec Middle East.*

December 11, 2019. https://cortec-me.com/
durability-the-cornerstone-of-sustainable-construction.

"Facade." *Cambridge Dictionary*. April 19, 2023. https://dictio-
nary.cambridge.org/us/dictionary/english/facade.

"Fears and Phobias (for Teens)." *Nemours KidsHealth*. 2023.
https://kidshealth.org/en/teens/phobias.html.

"Fighting your fears." *Better Health Channel*. 2021. https://
www.betterhealth.vic.gov.au/health/healthyliving/
Fighting-your-fears.

"Fort." *Vocabulary.com*. 2023. https://www.vocabulary.com/
dictionary/fort.

"Furniture." *International Standard Bible Encyclopedia Online*.
2023. https://www.internationalstandardbible.com/F/fur-
niture.html.

"Further Information on the Cenacle." *Cenacolo Vinciano*.
2023. https://cenacolovinciano.org/en/museum/
the-works/the-last-supper-leonardo-da-vinci-1452-1519.

Getlen, Larry. "How the Citicorp Center Nearly Toppled and
Other NYC Building Fiascos." *New York Post*. October 7,
2020. https://nypost.com/2020/10/07/how-the-citicorp-
center-nearly-toppled-and-other-nyc-building-fiascos.

"Getting to the Root of Tree Stability and Construction." *ILCA*.
Accessed January 6, 2020. https://www.bartlett.com/
resources/treestabilityandconstruction.pdf.

"Head & Shoulders First Impression 1991." YouTube. January 19, 2011. Video, :15. https://www.youtube.com/watch?v=1s9G4T0RPWo.

Hoffert, Josh. "Part 15: The Vine and the Branches." *Wind Ministries.* December 14, 2017. https://www.windministries.ca/blog/part-15-vine-branches.

"How Long Does Concrete Take to Dry?" *Dynamic Concrete Pumping Inc.* April 22, 2019. https://www.dcpu1.com/blog/how-long-does-concrete-take-to-dry.

Hughes, Bob. "City's Stately `Big John` Gets Off To A Tipsy Start." *Chicago Tribune.* March 24, 1985. https://www.chicagotribune.com/news/ct-xpm-1985-03-24-8501160598-story.html.

Iannucci, Lisa. "The Outer Shell Guide to Exterior Building Materials." *Cooperator News.* March 2014. https://cooperatornews.com/article/the-outer-shell.

"Insights on the Last Summer." *Cenacolo Vinciano.* 2023. https://cenacolovinciano.org/dentro-al-cenacolo.

"Machashabah." *Bible Study Tools.* 2023. https://www.biblestudytools.com/lexicons/hebrew/kjv/machashabah.html.

Moen, Skip Ph. D. "Cosmic Invention" *Hebrew Word Study.* July 23, 2010. https://skipmoen.com/2010/07/cosmic-invention.

Mote, Edward. "My Hope is Built on Nothing Less." (1835). *Hymnary.org.* Accessed January 6, 2021. https://hymnary.org/text/my_hope_is_built_on_nothing_less.

Motl, April. "What Is the Indwelling of the Holy Spirit?" *Christianity*. March 25, 2021. https://www.christianity. com/wiki/holy-spirit/what-is-the-indwelling-of-the-holy-spirit.html.

Newman, Randy. "Amazing Graces: How Complex the Sound!" *C.S. Lewis Institute*. March 4, 2018. https://www.cslewisinstitute.org/resources/ amazing-graces-how-complex-the-sound.

Oyekan, G.L., Prof. "Design of a 30 Storey Office Building With Reinforced Concrete ...." *PDFCoffee.com*. March 2014. https://pdfcoffee.com/design-of-a-30-storey-office-building-with-reinforced-concrete-design-using-etabs-structural-software-autosaved-pdf-free.html.

Philip, Alex. "Why are There no Chairs inside the Tabernacle?" *The Gospel Coalition*. March 14, 2018. https://ca.thegospel-coalition.org/article/no-chairs-inside-tabernacle.

"Review: Introduction to the Human Body." *SEER Training*. Accessed May 6, 2023. https://training.seer.cancer.gov/ anatomy/body/review.html.

"Safety Features in World's Tallest Building–Burj Khalifa." *Apaha*. June 15, 2019. https://apah.org.in/ safety-features-in-worlds-tallest-building-burj-khalifa.

Samsung C & T Global PR Manager. "Standing Tall: The Story Behind Skyscraper Foundations." *Samsung C & T*. April 13, 2018. https://news.samsungcnt.com/features/engi-neering-construction/2018-04-standing-tall-story-be-hind-skyscraper-foundations.

Shirer, Priscilla. *Discerning the Voice of God: How to Recognize When God Speaks*. Revised Edition. Chicago: Moody Publishers, 2017.

Smith, Randall. "Grasping God's Purpose: 'It's Time to Set the Table!' – Exodus 37:10 ...." *The Wandering Shepherd*. August 12, 2012. https://randalldsmith.com/grasping-gods-purpose-its-time-to-set-the-table.

Sony Pictures Home Entertainment. "A Movie Clip from The Natural." YouTube. May 15, 2018. Video, 3:12. https://www.youtube.com/watch?v=j-NdxwdSMns.

Stanley, Charles. "Being a Christian is Like Being an Onion." *Charles L. Stanley*. Accessed May 6, 2023. https://www.charleslstanley.com/being-a-christian-is-like-being-an-onion.

"The Importance of a Good Façade." *Bellmont Facade Engineering*. May 8, 2018. http://www.bellmont.net/blog/the-importance-of-a-good-facade.

"The world's tallest building, Burj Khalifa, is empty!?" *India Herald*. February 15, 2022. https://www.indiaherald.com/LifeStyle/Read/994476940/The-worlds-tallest-building-Burj-Khalifa-is-empty.

"Tony Evans–The Anointing." *Sermons.love*. Accessed May 6, 2023. https://sermons.love/tony-evans/13737-tony-evans-the-anointing.html .

Warren, Rick. "How to Use Your God-given Influence to Be a Kingdom Builder (Part 1)." *Pastors.com*. July 7, 2014. https://pastors.com/kingdom-builder-1/#:~:text=A%20

Kingdom%20b1uilder%20is%20on1e,every%20
step%aof20the%2a0way.

"We The Kingdom–God Is On The Throne (Live From
Franni's House)." Youtube. September 11, 2022. Video,
2:54. https://www.youtube.com/watch?v=y9Xj-g7aJ0A.

Wood, Bryant. "The walls of Jericho." *Creation Ministries
International.* March 1999. https://creation.com/
the-walls-of-jericho.

Yiu, Kayla. "Reclining at the Table With Jesus." *In Touch
Ministries.* March 16, 2022. https://www.intouch.org/read/
articles/reclining-at-the-table-with-jesus.

Notes

Chapter 1: His Plans
1. "Machashabah," Bible Study Tools, 2023, https://www.biblestudytools.com/lexicons/hebrew/kjv/machashabah.html.
2. Skip Moen Ph.D., "Cosmic Invention," Hebrew Word Study, July 23, 2010, https://skipmoen.com/2010/07/cosmic-invention.

Chapter 2: Preparation
Photo used with permission of Nancy Padan
3. Craig Collins, "The Overview Effect," Issuu, accessed March 6, 2020, https://issuu.com/faircountmedia/docs/international_20space_20station_2020_20years_20of_/s/11253985.

Chapter 3: A Strong Foundation
Photo used with permission of Staci Tryon
4. Bob Hughes, "City's Stately `Big John` Gets Off To A Tipsy Start," Chicago Tribune, March 24, 1985, https://www.chicagotribune.com/news/ct-xpm-1985-03-24-8501160598-story.html.
5. Ibid.

6. Prof. G.L. Oyekan, "Design of a 30 Storey Office Building With Reinforced Concrete (Autosaved)," PDFCoffee.com, March 2014, https://pdfcoffee.com/design-of-a-30-storey-office-building-with-reinforced-concrete-design-using-etabs-structural-software-autosaved-pdf-free.html.

7. Bob Hughes, "City's Stately `Big John` Gets Off To A Tipsy Start," Chicago Tribune, March 24, 1985, https://www.chicagotribune.com/news/ct-xpm-1985-03-24-8501160598-story.html.

8. Ibid.

9. "Getting to the Root of Tree Stability and Construction," ILCA, accessed January 6, 2020, https://www.bartlett.com/resources/treestabilityandconstruction.pdf.

10. "About Coast Redwoods," California Department of Parks and RecreationState, accessed January 6, 2020, https://www.parks.ca.gov/?page_id=22257.

11. Edward Mote, "My Hope is Built on Nothing Less," (1835), Hymnary.org, accessed January 6, 2021, https://hymnary.org/text/my_hope_is_built_on_nothing_less.
Photo used with permission of Carla Wehrmeyer

Chapter 4: Fortification
Photo used with permission of Mark Bennett
Name was changed to Ms. Beverly

12. Jackie Craven, "Safe Rooms and Shelters–What You Need to Know," ThoughtCo, September 25, 2018, https://www.thoughtco.com/safe-room-what-is-a-safe-room-177327.

13. Samsung C & T Global PR Manager, "Standing Tall: The Story Behind Skyscraper Foundations," Samsung C & T Newsroom, April 13, 2018, https://news.samsungcnt.com/features/

engineering-construction/2018-04-standing-tall-story-be-hind-skyscraper-foundations.

14. Larry Getlen, "How the Citicorp Center Nearly Toppled and Other NYC Building Fiascos," New York Post, October 7, 2020, https://nypost.com/2020/10/07/how-the-citicorp-center-nearly-toppled-and-other-nyc-building-fiascos.

15. Samsung C & T Global PR Manager, "Standing Tall: The Story Behind Skyscraper Foundations," Samsung C & T, April 13, 2018, https://news.samsungcnt.com/features/engineering-construction/2018-04-standing-tall-story-be-hind-skyscraper-foundations.

16. "Fort." Vocabulary.com. 2023. https://www.vocabulary.com/dictionary/fort.

17. "Casting Crowns–Just Be Held (Live)," YouTube, January 27, 2016, video, 3:43, https://www.youtube.com/watch?v=s53R3aj5pfc.

Chapter 5: Stress Test

18. "How Long Does Concrete Take to Dry?" Dynamic Concrete Pumping Inc., April 22, 2019, https://www.dcpu1.com/blog/how-long-does-concrete-take-to-dry.

19. "Break Tests or Maturity Method?" Maturix, March 11, 2021, https://maturix.com/knowledge-center/break-tests-vs-maturity-method.

20. "5 challenges faced while building Dubai's Burj Khalifa," Khaleej Times, Accessed January 4, 2019, https://www.khaleejtimes.com/uae/5-challenges-faced-while-building-dubais-burj-khalifa.

21. "The world's tallest building, Burj Khalifa, is empty!?" India Herald, February 15, 2022, https://

www.indiaherald.com/LifeStyle/Read/994476940/
The-worlds-tallest-building-Burj-Khalifa-is-empty.

22. "Durability: The Cornerstone of Sustainable
    Construction!" Cortec Middle East,
    December 11, 2019, https://cortec-me.com/
    durability-the-cornerstone-of-sustainable-construction.

23. "Safety Features in World's Tallest Building–Burj
    Khalifa," Apaha, June 15, 2019, https://apah.org.in/
    safety-features-in-worlds-tallest-building-burj-khalifa.

24. "Danny Gokey–Stay Strong (Official Music Video),"
    YouTube, February 10, 2023, video, 3:18, https://www.you-
    tube.com/watch?v=TY-jh4RS_I0.

Chapter 6: Razing Wall, Raising Walls

25. Bryant Wood, "The walls of Jericho." Creation Ministries
    International, March 1999, https://creation.com/
    the-walls-of-jericho.

26. Ibid.

27. Ibid.

28. Ibid.

29. Ibid.

30. Pricilla Shirer, Discerning the Voice of God: How to
    Recognize When God Speaks. Revised Edition. (Chicago:
    Moody Publishers, 2017), 136.

Chapter 7: The Power Source

Photo used with permission of Mark Bennett

32. Mark Bendix, "Electrical Design for Tall
    Buildings," Consulting–Specifying Engineer,
    August 1, 2007, https://www.csemag.com/articles/
    electrical-design-for-tall-buildings.

33. "Review: Introduction to the Human Body," SEER Training, Accessed May 6, 2023, https://training.seer.cancer.gov/anatomy/body/review.html.

34. "Andrea Bocelli Talks About His Strong Faith in God," EWTN News In-Depth, Youtube, April 10, 2021, video,11:13, https://youtu.be/oN_FVhfZEPw.

35. Ibid.

36. Josh Hoffert, "Part 15: The Vine and the Branches," Wind Ministries, December 14, 2017, https://www.windministries.ca/blog/part-15-vine-branches.

37. Sony Pictures Home Entertainment, The Natural, Youtube, May 15, 2018. video, 3:12. https://www.youtube.com/watch?v=lAoHN4xC_7c.

Chapter 8: Our Facade

38. "Head & Shoulders First Impression 1991," YouTube, January 19, 2011, video, :15, https://www.youtube.com/watch?v=1s9G4T0RPWo.

39. Lisa Iannucci, "The Importance of a Good Façade," Bellmont Facade Engineering, May 8, 2018, http://www.bellmont.net/blog/the-importance-of-a-good-facade.

40. Charles Stanley, "Being a Christian is Like Being an Onion," Charles L. Stanley, Accessed May 6, 2023, https://www.charleslstanley.com/being-a-christian-is-like-being-an-onion.

41. "Facade," Cambridge English Dictionary, April 19, 2023, https://dictionary.cambridge.org/us/dictionary/english/facade.

42. Charles Stanley, "Being a Christian is Like Being an Onion," Charles L. Stanley, Accessed

May 6, 2023, https://www.charleslstanley.com/being-a-christian-is-like-being-an-onion.

43. David Roger Clawson M.D., "What You Need to Know About Spiritual Illness and Disease," Psychology Today, March 20, 2021, https://www.psychology-today.com/sg/blog/deconstructing-illness/202103/what-you-need-know-about-spiritual-illness-and-disease.

44. Lisa Iannucci, "The Outer Shell Guide to Exterior Building Materials," Cooperator News, March 2014, https://cooper-atornews.com/article/the-outer-shell.

45. David Roger Clawson M.D., "What You Need to Know About Spiritual Illness and Disease," Psychology Today, March 20, 2021, https://www.psychology-today.com/sg/blog/deconstructing-illness/202103/what-you-need-know-about-spiritual-illness-and-disease.

46. Ibid.

47. Lisa Iannucci, "The Outer Shell Guide to Exterior Building Materials," Cooperator News, March 2014, https://cooper-atornews.com/article/the-outer-shell.

Chapter 9: Simple Furnishings

48. "Furniture." International Standard Bible Encyclopedia. 2023. https://www.internationalstandardbible.com/F/furniture.html.

49. Jura Concius, "How to furnish, fill and decorate your new, larger home," Washington Post, September 21, 2021, https://www.washingtonpost.com/home/2021/09/21/how-to-furnish-decorate-upsize-home.

50. Sony Pictures Home Entertainment, The Natural, Youtube, May 15, 2018, 3:12, https://www.youtube.com/watch?v=j-NdxwdSMns&t=12s.

51. Randall Smith, "Grasping God's Purpose: 'It's Time to Set the Table!' – Exodus 37:10 …," The Wandering Shepherd, August 12, 2012, https://randalldsmith.com/grasping-gods-purpose-its-time-to-set-the-table.

52. "Insights on the Last Supper," Cenacolo Vinciano, 2023, https://cenacolovinciano.org/en/museum/the-works/the-last-supper-leonardo-da-vinci-1452-1519.

53. Kayla Yiu, "Reclining at the Table With Jesus," In Touch Ministries, March 16, 2022, https://www.intouch.org/read/articles/reclining-at-the-table-with-jesus.

54. Ibid.

55. Alex Philip, "Why are There no Chairs inside the Tabernacle?" The Gospel Coalition, March 14, 2018, https://ca.thegospelcoalition.org/article/no-chairs-inside-tabernacle.

56. Ibid.

57. "We The Kingdom–God Is On The Throne (Live From Franni's House)," Youtube, September 11, 2022, video, 4:50, https://www.youtube.com/watch?v=y9Xj-g7aJ0A.

Chapter 10: The Spirit Inside

58. April Motl,"What Is the Indwelling of the Holy Spirit?" Christianity, March 25, 2021, https://www.christianity.com/wiki/holy-spirit/what-is-the-indwelling-of-the-holy-spirit.html.

59. Ibid.

60. Ibid.

61. Randy Newman, "Amazing Graces: How Complex the Sound!" C.S. Lewis Institute, March 4, 2018, https://www.cslewisinstitute.org/resources/amazing-graces-how-complex-the-sound.

62. "Tony Evans–The Anointing," Sermons.love, Accessed May 6, 2023, https://sermons.love/tony-evans/13737-tony-evans-the-anointing.html.
63. Ibid.

Chapter 11: Maintenance Agreement
Photo used with permission of Mark Bennett
64. "Fears and Phobias (for Teens)," Nemours KidsHealth, 2023, https://kidshealth.org/en/teens/phobias.html.
65. "Fighting your fears," Better Health Channel, 2021, https://www.betterhealth.vic.gov.au/health/healthyliving/Fighting-your-fears.
Photos used with permission of Emily Bennett

Conclusion: But Until Then…
Price, Rebekah MSN, APRN, FNP-C. Conversation used with permission. August 2, 2023.

Author
Headshot taken by Lilly Isabella Photography

Acknowledgement
66. Rick Warren, "How to Use Your God-given Influence to Be a Kingdom Builder (Part 1)," Pastors.com, July 7, 2014, https://pastors.com/kingdom-builder-1/#:~a:text=A%20Kingdom%20b1uilder%20is%20on1e,every%20step%aof20the%2a0way.

Teri Bennett's First Published Book

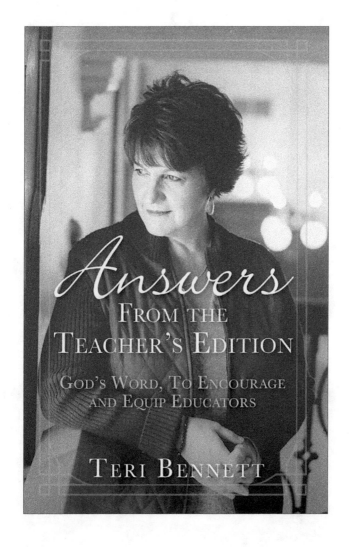

Printed in the USA
CPSIA information can be obtained
at www.ICGtesting.com
JSHW011042201123
52350JS00006B/18